T0086099

BAPTISM

**See also these titles in the
Christian Essentials Series**

The Ten Commandments
by Peter J. Leithart

The Apostles' Creed
by Ben Myers

The Lord's Prayer
by Wesley Hill

BAPTISM

A Guide to Life from Death

PETER J. LEITHART

LEXHAM PRESS

CHRISTIAN ESSENTIALS

Baptism: A Guide to Life from Death
Christian Essentials

Copyright 2021 Peter Leithart

Lexham Press, 1313 Commercial St., Bellingham, WA 98225
LexhamPress.com

Print ISBN 9781683594635
Digital ISBN 9781683594642
Library of Congress Number 2020951962

Series Editor: Todd Hains
Lexham Editorial: Matthew Boffey, Abigail Stocker, Abigail Salinger
Cover Design: Eleazar Ruiz
Typesetting: Fanny Palacios, Abigail Stocker

Praise for *Baptism*

Peter Leithart is one of our best theological writers, and he has given us here a fresh, finely textured study of the sacrament of baptism. A book of liturgical wisdom for all of God's people—wherever their place may be in the Lord's family.

Timothy George
distinguished professor,
Beeson Divinity School of Samford University

I have always enjoyed reading the writing of Peter Leithart, even when I disagree. He is a wordsmith in the truest sense of that term. This new work on baptism is true to form: crisp, pellucid, and provocative. Given my proclivities for Particular Baptist baptismal thought of the long eighteenth century, there is much here with which I agree, though I am forced to exclaim at times in reading his passionate prose: if this be true, the circle of baptism must be drawn at believers! Despite such dissent, I strongly recommend this small work: it compels deep and profitable thinking about what has long been a controverted subject.

Michael A. G. Haykin
professor of church history,
The Southern Baptist Theological Seminary

In this wonderful book, Leithart discovers in the baptismal font the confluence of many streams of scriptural narrative and testimony, streams united in Christ and poured out in his Spirit upon his church. Caught up in the mighty current of these waters, readers will be more powerfully driven forward in their worship and work.

Alastair Roberts
scholar, Theopolis Institute,
Davenant Institute, *Mere Fidelity* podcast;
author of *Echoes of Exodus*

It's hard to find enough superlatives to extol this rich catechesis for the baptized people of God. Unfortunately, baptism is the source of much division among Christians. Yet in this marvelous little book Leithart gives us much to ponder. Chock-full of scripture and sprinkled with scintillating quotes from the church fathers, this remarkable book is a poetic paean to the wonders of what it means to be baptized in the name of the Father, Son, and Holy Spirit.

I found a few things to quibble about. Infant baptism need not automatically include infant communion, for example. Less sacramental Christians will find other objections too, no doubt.

Still, this book is an incredible gift to us all and will greatly enhance the ongoing conversation about our one Lord, one faith, one baptism (Eph 4:5). Take, read, and rejoice in all the gifts God gives you in your baptism!

Harold L. Senkbeil
executive director emeritus,
DOXOLOGY: The Lutheran Center for Spiritual Care and Counsel;
author of *The Care of Souls: Cultivating a Pastor's Heart*

Peter Leithart's theology is always bracing, fresh, a fresh blast that drives out the stale air that theology is used to. But this book is also gentle, pastoral, accessible. Leithart is always erudite and wise, yet here he is also accessible to any of the baptized or anyone considering baptism. This is a brilliant resource for the classroom with your best university students or for teenagers contemplating new life in Christ. For it is not just about baptism. It is about the triune God, about the whole of the Christian faith, and about how to be more human.

Jason Byassee
Butler Chair in Homiletics and Biblical Interpretation,
The Vancouver School of Theology;
author of *Surprised by Jesus Again*

To Dr. Paul Leithart,
1921–2019
Beloved Physician

CONTENTS

CHRISTIAN ESSENTIALS

SERIES PREFACE

he Christian Essentials series passes down tradition that matters.

The church has often spoken paradoxically about growth in Christian faith: to grow means to stay at the beginning. The great Reformer Martin Luther exemplified this. "Although I'm indeed an old doctor," he said, "I never move on from the childish doctrine of the Ten Commandments and the Apostles' Creed and the Lord's Prayer. I still daily learn and pray them with my little Hans and my little Lena." He had just as much to learn about the Lord as his children.

The ancient church was founded on basic biblical teachings and practices like the Ten Commandments, baptism, the Apostles' Creed, the Lord's Supper, the Lord's Prayer, and corporate worship. These basics of the Christian life have sustained and nurtured every generation of the faithful—from the apostles to today. They apply equally to old and young, men and women, pastors and church members. "In Christ Jesus you are all sons of God through faith" (Gal 3:26).

We need the wisdom of the communion of saints. They broaden our perspective beyond our current culture and time. "Every age has its own outlook," C. S. Lewis wrote. "It is specially good at seeing certain truths and specially liable to make certain mistakes." By focusing on what's current, we rob ourselves of the insights and questions of those who have gone before us. On the other hand, by reading our forebears in faith, we engage ideas that otherwise might never occur to us.

The books in the Christian Essentials series open up the meaning of the foundations of our faith. These basics are unfolded afresh for today in conversation with the great tradition—grounded in and strengthened by Scripture—for the continuing growth of all the children of God.

> *Hear, O Israel: The Lord our God, the Lord is one. You shall love the Lord your God with all your heart and with all your soul and with all your might. And these words that I command you today shall be on your heart. You shall teach them diligently to your children, and shall talk of them when you sit in your house, and when you walk by the way, and when you lie down, and when you rise. You shall bind them as a sign on your hand, and they shall be as frontlets between your eyes. You shall write them on the doorposts of your house and on your gates.* (Deuteronomy 6:4–9)

ALMIGHTY AND ETERNAL GOD,

who through the flood, according to your righteous judgment, condemned the unfaithful world, and according to your great mercy, saved faithful Noah, even eight persons,

and has drowned hard-hearted Pharaoh with all his army in the Red Sea, and has led your people Israel dry through it,

thereby prefiguring this bath of your holy baptism,

and through the baptism of your dear child, our Lord Jesus Christ, has sanctified and set apart the Jordan and all water for a saving flood,

and an ample washing away of sins:

we pray that through your same infinite mercy you would graciously look down upon this your child, and bless her with a right faith in the Spirit,

so that through this saving flood all that was born in her from Adam and all which she has added thereto might be drowned and submerged;

and that she may be separated from the unfaithful, and preserved in the holy ark of Christendom dry and safe, and may be ever fervent in spirit and joyful in hope to serve your name,

so that she with all the faithful may be worthy to inherit your promise of eternal life, through Christ Jesus our Lord.

AMEN.

ALMIGHTY AND ETERNAL GOD

I

FAMILY, BODY, TEMPLE

"Worthy to inherit your promise of eternal life."

 alk about baptism, and you're immediately plunged into arguments. *Whom* should we baptize—professing converts or infants? *How* should we baptize—by immersion, pouring, or sprinkling? *Why* do we baptize—as a sign of God's claim or as a convert's public confession of faith? *What* does baptism do—nothing, something, everything? If it does something, *how long* does it last—for a moment, forever?[1]

All Christians use water to baptize. All invoke the Triune name. Beyond that, there's little consensus. Quarrels over baptism are a travesty. The church has one baptism, as it is one body with one Spirit, one Lord, one hope, one faith, and one Father (Eph 4:4–6). Yet God's sign of unity is a spring of division. We're Corinthians, acting as if we were baptized into the

1

name of Thomas or Calvin or Luther or John Piper (1 Cor 1:10–18). Paul's outrage echoes down the centuries: "Is Christ divided?"

This book is a small contribution to the effort to reunite a church divided by baptism. My approach is oblique. I don't offer any nice knock-down arguments. As currently framed, the controversies are insoluble anyway. To arrive at unity, we need to recover the baptismal imagination of earlier generations. We need to start at the foundation and work our way up.

The building blocks of that foundation are neatly laid out by Luther's Great Flood Prayer, which I've long used whenever I perform a baptism:

> Almighty and eternal God, who through the flood, according to your righteous judgment, condemned the unfaithful world, and according to your great mercy, saved faithful Noah, even eight persons, and has drowned hard-hearted Pharaoh with all his army in the Red Sea, and has led your people Israel dry through it, thereby prefiguring this bath of your holy baptism, and through the baptism of your dear child, our Lord Jesus Christ, has sanctified and set apart the Jordan and all water for a saving flood, and an ample washing away of sins: we pray that through your same infinite mercy you would graciously look down upon this your child, and bless her with a right faith in the spirit, so that through this saving flood all that was born in her from Adam

and all which she has added thereto might be drowned and submerged; and that she may be separated from the unfaithful, and preserved in the holy ark of Christendom dry and safe, and may be ever fervent in spirit and joyful in hope to serve your name, so that she with all the faithful may be worthy to inherit your promise of eternal life, through Christ Jesus our Lord. Amen.[2]

For biblical breadth, Luther's prayer is hard to match. He links baptism with Adam's sin, the flood, the exodus, and Jesus' baptism.[3] According to Luther, baptism does an awful lot: it separates us from the unfaithful and preserves us in the church; it washes, delivers, judges, and saves.

Some Christians will be dismayed at the power Luther attributes to baptism, taking it as evidence that the great German Reformer didn't quite purge Catholicism from his soul. But Luther's prayer expresses the mainstream convictions of two millennia of Christian tradition. Western Catholics, Eastern Orthodox, and many Protestants say exactly these things about baptism.

The church says these things because Scripture does. The Bible speaks of baptism as an *effective* rite: baptism brands us with the Triune name (Matt 28:18–20); washes sin (Acts 2:38a); confers the Spirit (Acts 2:39b); grafts us into Jesus' death, burial, and resurrection (Rom 6:1–14); justifies (Rom 6:7); sanctifies (1 Cor 6:11); joins us with the Spirit-filled body (1 Cor 12:12–13); clothes us with Christ (Gal 3:27–29); regenerates (Titus 3:5);

3

and saves (1 Pet 3:21). By baptism, we are anointed as priests and kings and join the Pentecostal company of prophets (Acts 2:15–21, 37–42). Baptized into one name, we become members of one another (1 Cor 1:10–18; Eph 4:4–6). The Bible never portrays baptism as a picture of some more important event that happens without baptism. What baptism pictures happens—at baptism. Baptism *works*.

If we're uncomfortable with what Christians have said about baptism, it's because we don't share their convictions about the church. Nearly all errors and confusions about baptism are errors and confusions about the church. At the outset, let me lay out three basic beliefs that are implicit in Luther's prayer and provide the structural support for our study of baptism.[4]

First, human beings are created as social beings. If we are saved as humans, we must be saved as social creatures. Salvation must take form as a saved society, a community delivered from the wounds of ambition, fear, hatred, envy, and greed. The church is the community God has delivered, and continues to deliver, from evil desires, habits, and imaginations, as we make our way to a final deliverance. Sinners are out of tune with God, creation, and one another. The church is humanity restored to harmony. The church is salvation in social form.

The New Testament describes the church as the family of the Father, the body of the incarnate Son, the temple of the Holy Spirit. These descriptions are simply *true*. We members of the church are—without any ifs, ands, or buts—sons and daughters of our heavenly Father, objects of his loving care and discipline. Jesus is no longer present in his personal body, but the church is—without any ifs, ands, or buts—his corporate body. Jesus is still available to the world through the church. Jesus and the church form one thing—"Christ" (1 Cor 12:12), what Augustine called "the whole Christ" (Latin, *totus Christus*). Jesus acts through us by his Spirit, making us his hands, feet, eyes, ears, and heart. The Spirit animates a living temple in which every member—without any ifs, ands, or buts—is a living stone. This is most certainly true.

Some children abandon their Father. Fruitless branches are pruned from the vine. Stubborn sinners so grieve the Spirit that he abandons them. They betray *as* children, atrophy *as* organs of the body, choose death *as* living stones of the temple. The mystifying tragedy of such traitors doesn't change the fact that they once communed with the Triune God.

Second, by his resurrection and ascension Jesus burst through death into the life of the age to come. He's the last Adam, clothed with eternal glory, overflowing with life. Because the church is the body of the last Adam, she shares the life of Jesus. Eternal life erupts into the world through the church. "Whoever is in Christ, behold a new creation!" Paul says (2 Cor 5:17, my translation). By the Spirit, the church is "in Christ." We have not yet entered fully into the new creation; we strain with the Spirit for creation's liberation from its bondage to decay. Yet, even now, filled with the Spirit of Jesus, the pledge of our inheritance (Eph 1:14), the church is a whisper of final harmony in a dissonant world.

We think the unalterable past enslaves us, but the gospel scrambles the relation of past and future. Our future isn't determined by the fall of Adam or the sins of our past. In Christ, God has opened a future determined solely by his promises. On pilgrimage toward new Jerusalem, we already taste the delights of the destination. We are who God's word says we are. We are now who we will be.

Third, followers of Jesus participate in rites, signs, and sacraments.[5] Communion with the Triune God doesn't take place primarily in a hermit's cell, in the inner chambers of the heart, or in a flight above the sky. Communion takes place in public, communal rituals. The church is a human (and divine) society, and, as Augustine said, every society is knit together by signs.[6] Of course, God can save people without baptism or the Lord's Supper,[7] but the Christian life normally revolves around liturgical rites or signs—baptism, Eucharist, common prayer, confession and absolution, song, reading and hearing Scripture. Someone who says he follows Jesus but never bathes in baptism or eats at the Lord's Table isn't a member of Christ's body. He's not a Christian, no matter what he says. Christians get a taste of the life to come in the places God designates through the words, liturgies, signs, and rites of the whole Christ. Observe a baptism, a sermon, a Eucharist, and you're seeing human beings sharing the life of new creation, which is the very life of God.

These three beliefs hang together. The church is the family of the Father, the body of the Son, and the temple of the Spirit because it shares in the new creation that has begun in Jesus. And the church shares in that new creation by hearing the word, confessing sin, assembling at the Lord's Table, passing through the waters of baptism.

Keep this in mind as we move ahead. Baptism is the doorway into membership in the church. Whenever I say, "Baptism does X," remember what I've said about the church. Big things happen at baptism, but baptism's energy doesn't sputter to a halt as soon as we dry off. Baptism is powerful because it places us in the church where pastors, friends, and mentors train us and pray for us—where God corrects and feeds us by his word at his table. Baptism does what it does because Jesus authorizes it. Baptism works because the *church* works, and the church works because it's the body of Christ, enlivened by the Spirit.

If the church is what the New Testament says it is and if baptism is the doorway to the church, then certain things necessarily follow: baptism is adoption into the Father's family, union with Christ in his body, installation as a living stone in the temple of the Spirit. If the church is what the New Testament claims, baptism gives us a share in the resurrection life of the Son and his Spirit. If the church is as the New Testament describes it, baptism is the gift of a future, propelling us toward the unending joys of a new heaven and a new earth. It is indeed, a "saving flood."

WHO THROUGH THE FLOOD,
ACCORDING TO
YOUR RIGHTEOUS JUDGMENT,
CONDEMNED THE UNFAITHFUL WORLD,
AND ACCORDING TO YOUR GREAT MERCY,
SAVED FAITHFUL NOAH,
EVEN EIGHT PERSONS

II

RITES OLD AND NEW

"Prefiguring this bath of your holy baptism."

B aptism is a sign. We grasp what it signifies when we locate baptism in the flow of biblical history. If we want to renew our baptismal imagination, we need to be immersed in Scripture.

The apostles read the Old Testament as a preview of Jesus, full of blurry snapshots of the coming Savior. Jesus is the last Adam (Rom 5:12–21). He's the seed of Abraham, a resurrected Isaac (Heb 11:17–19), the living temple of God (John 1:14; 2:13–22), the son of David (Rom 1:1–4), a prophet like Moses who leads his people in a new exodus from the Egypt of sin and death (Luke 9:31; Acts 3:22; 7:37). Jesus is the key to all the puzzling riddles of the Old Testament. The second-century Greek bishop Irenaeus used a beautiful image to explain this: the Old Testament contains the fragments of a mosaic; when you put all the pieces together, the mosaic portrays the face of a handsome prince, Jesus, the Prince of Peace.[8] The church fathers called the Old Testament fragments "types" (from the Greek, *typoi*) and saw Jesus as the fulfillment or "antitype" that pulled all the pieces together.[9]

This has everything to do with baptism. Jesus' baptism is the primary baptism. In a sense, it is the one and only baptism. Every other baptism unites us to the baptism of Jesus. That's why the apostles found blurry snapshots of baptism in the Old Testament, along with snapshots of Jesus. Like Jesus himself, baptism gathers together all the great events and characters of the Bible. Baptism makes us living epistles of God, full of his living words.

Baptism is the reality prefigured by the waters of creation and Eden, Noah's flood (1 Pet 3:18–22), and Israel's exodus through the sea (1 Cor 10:1–5). The church fathers found types of baptism in Joshua's river-passage into Canaan, Elijah's drenched sacrifice, Elisha's floating axe head, the cleansing of the Syrian commander Naaman, and Jesus' healing of the lame man at Bethsaida and of the man born blind.[10] Jesus arranges all the shiny fragments of the mosaic into a beautiful picture. When we're baptized to become members of the "whole Christ," all the pieces of Jesus' portrait become part of our portrait. All the types that prefigure Jesus also prefigure the baptized.

A ugustine explains the distinction between the old and new covenants with a grammatical illustration. Using the future tense, we say, "The Messiah will be raised." In the perfect tense, we say, "The Messiah has been raised." The root word is identical; the two phrases refer to the same reality. In Latin, the ending is the only thing that changes, but that tiny alteration of form generates a momentous shift in meaning, the difference between "I *hope* for a new life" and "I've *started* a new life."[11]

Biblical rites are like root words of a language. All of them share a common meaning. All of them signify God's promises, which are fulfilled in Jesus. Jesus is the meaning of every biblical ritual, but the form of the rituals varies with the times. As a future-tense rite, circumcision signified Israel's hope for the Messiah's advent and triumph. As a present-tense sign, baptism announces the Messiah has come. Jesus is the word of promise, conjugated by the rites of Israel and the church.

Baptism is a present-tense sign of the gospel, the good news that Irenaeus's prince has arrived in the world. And so baptism makes a claim about the world. It tells us we don't live in the world of Abraham, Moses, David, or Jeremiah. We live in a new world and a new time, the world of King Jesus, who rules in the age we call AD (*Anno Domini*, "Year of our Lord"). The mere fact that Christian baptism cascades over planet Earth tells us something has happened to the world, the happening we call Jesus. Baptism shouts, "The time is fulfilled! The kingdom has come!" It tells us that Jesus and the Spirit have completed, and are completing, all that the Father promised (2 Cor 1:20–22), restoring the world to the harmony of peace. Baptism is the sign of all of this. It heralds a new time.

Baptism doesn't just *picture* an announcement. Baptism *announces*. It doesn't portray preaching; it preaches. Prophets compared the coming kingdom to a bursting spring of living water (Isa 44:3), a flood of gentiles bearing gifts (Isa 66:12), a cleansing fountain (Zech 13:1). As baptismal water gushes across the globe, God declares these promises fulfilled. Baptism *is* the gospel, good news from a distant land (Prov 25:25).[12]

Baptism preaches because it's God's work. Baptism isn't simply water, nor water poured, nor water over which a Trinitarian formula is intoned. Baptism is an act of the church, using water in the name of the Trinity to bathe a person entering the church. Because Jesus commands baptism, it is an act of God.[13] The hand that dunks or pours is the hand of the minister, but the Spirit baptizes us into the one body (1 Cor 12:12–13). When the rite is done, the baptized person isn't just wet. He or she is *baptized*, by God. At every baptism, God himself preaches the good news of his Son. Every baptized person is a fresh announcement of God's promise, commissioned to proclaim the good news.

Baptism preaches whether or not anyone believes it. God heralds good news at every baptism. Baptism is a ritual clock. It tells the world's time—"The kingdom is come! The time is fulfilled!"—even if no one sets his watch by it. Baptism does what it's designed to do—announcing the new time of the gospel—simply by being done.[14]

B aptism is more than an announcement. It's an effective announcement. Christians have always denied that baptism is a mere or empty sign. No "naked signs," Reformer John Calvin insists.[15] As God preaches in baptism, he makes the gospel visible, earthly, and real.

Let's think about this by considering circumcision. Yahweh told Abraham to circumcise the males of his household as bearers of promise (Gen 17:9–27). By circumcision and covenant, Abraham's family were separated from the nations and promised gifts of land and seed, so that Abraham's family would eventually bless the nations (Gen 12:1–3). At every circumcision, Israel's vocation was inscribed in flesh.

Jesus fulfills Yahweh's promise to Abraham. He shatters the wall between Jew and gentile (Eph 2:11–22), so that God's blessing immerses the nations. Baptism doesn't just picture what Jesus has done in uniting Jews and gentiles in one body. Baptism unites them. Every converted Jew is washed; every converted gentile is washed. Every man is washed, and every woman. At baptism, the Spirit knits all peoples into one body, blessed with the blessing of Abraham (Eph 4:4–6). The good news of Jesus, who fulfills the promise to Abraham, comes true at every baptism.

By the same token, baptism doesn't announce a new priesthood somewhere. It is an initiation rite for priests, and it *forms* the priesthood. Baptism doesn't just portray a new Israel following a new Joshua into battle; it musters the new-Israel army.[16] Through baptism (and preaching, confession and absolution, the Supper, and the communion of saints), the gospel takes a local habitation. Through baptism, salvation takes form as the church. Baptism retunes discordant humanity. Every baptism proclaims good news to the world and makes that good news real.

Baptism is, of course, good news to baptized individuals—the good news of forgiveness, cleansing, justification, sanctification, and glorification. For individuals, as for the world, baptism is a sign, but it's more than a sign. That "more" is often captured by the term "seal."[17] A seal is a mark of ownership and identity. None of us is autonomous. As our very names attest, we all belong to someone. A seal tells us who we are by telling us to whom we belong. Early Christians compared the "seal" (Greek, *sphragis*) of baptism to a brand on an animal,[18] a mark on a slave,[19] or a regimental tattoo on a Roman soldier.[20] Sealed with the Triune name, the baptized belongs to the Triune God. God seals him or her as a member of the flock of God, a servant in the Father's house, a warrior under the command of King Jesus.

Baptism tells us we don't belong to ourselves (1 Cor 6:19–20), but it doesn't merely *tell* us. It makes it so. In baptism, God redeems us from the devil's prison to the free family of Jesus and raises us from the grave to resurrection life. Baptism is a transfer of ownership from the world to the church.

Seals impose demands. Sheep must follow the shepherd. Slaves obey their master. Soldiers must be ready to fight and die. Seals are also promises. Good shepherds care for their sheep. Good masters love their slaves. Good generals provide for their troops. Sealed with baptism, we are taken from the old and brought into the new. As baptism announces the gospel, it plunges the baptized into the reality of the gospel. Because baptism seals, it saves, because belonging to God *is* being saved.

AND HAS DROWNED
HARD-HEARTED PHARAOH
WITH ALL HIS ARMY IN THE RED SEA,
AND HAS LED YOUR PEOPLE ISRAEL
DRY THROUGH IT

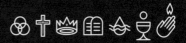

III

WORLD FROM WATER

"Our Lord Jesus Christ has sanctified
… all water for a saving flood."

esus initiates a new creation in the midst of the old:
"Whoever is in Christ, behold, a new creation!"
(2 Cor 5:17, my translation). After his resurrection,
Jesus no longer lives the life of the old Adam, who was "from
the earth" (1 Cor 15:47). Jesus is the last Adam, the heavenly
man, raised with a Spiritual body. Jesus *is* the new creation, but
he's the head of a body. All his members share the resurrection
life of the age to come (Heb 6:5).[21] Jesus is the new creation in
person.

"What time is it?" we ask. Baptism answers, "The time of
Jesus, which means the time of new creation." Why would
God use water to announce the new creation? Read the first

few pages of the Bible, and you'll find out. God is himself a "fountain of living water" (Jer 2:13), so it's no surprise that the first creation is born of water and the Spirit.[22] Yahweh creates an empty void, a "deep" of waters (Gen 1:1–2), the Spirit's "throne" and "chariot."[23] He hauls water to the sky and sets a firmament-dam to separate waters above and below (Gen 1:6–8). He divides the waters below to expose dry land (Gen 1:9–10). Living souls first fill the sea (Gen 1:20–23). The second-century theologian Tertullian notes that the waters were "commanded to bring forth living things," and asks, Is it any wonder that "waters already know how to make alive"?[24] Ambrose, fourth-century bishop of Milan, draws a similar connection: "the waters should regenerate you into grace, even as those other waters generated into life," which leads him to the exhortation, "Imitate the fish."[25]

Each zone of creation has a unique form of water. Before heaven's throne is a sea of glass like crystal (Rev 4:6). Land is crossed by rivers and dappled with lakes. Oceans cover 70 percent of Earth's surface, and water flows in a vast network of underground channels and lakes.[26] From top to bottom, our planet is a water world. "Christ is never without water," says Tertullian.[27] We may also say: creation is never without water.

Water is "just" H_2O, but it fills our senses. Brooks burble, rain plops and patters, tides roar in and out, and water sounds send us to sleep. The sun pinks morning clouds, purples them at evening, and shows off by turning drops into colored bows. Is there anything so refreshing as a warm bath, a dip in the pool, a glass of iced water on a sweltering afternoon? Rime glorifies spider webs, and snow sparkles the dingiest landscape. Does anything smell of life like soil soaked with spring showers or the dank dark sea? Arid lands are barren wombs without the seed of rain (Isa 55:10), and the water cycle regulates weather. The living world is a "partnership between biological molecules and water."[28] Without the right water in the right proportions, earth would still be "formless and void." God demonstrates his goodness with a lavish gift of water.

In fact, *we* are watery. As the Syrian writer Narsai said, "The nature of Adam's clay the Creator took and fashioned it in water and heated it in the Spirit; and it acquired beauty."[29] We're roughly 60 percent water, nearly as liquid as Earth. Your brain is more than half water. Digestive juices—saliva, bile, mucus—are mostly water, and intercellular and extra-cellular exchanges take place through water. Blood is mostly water, as are semen and breast milk.[30] Where would we be if water were not a nearly universal solvent?[31] In the hospital, or dead. We're microcosms, small water worlds. Can baptism mean anything less than "new creation" and "new life"?

Paradise, too, was a "well-watered place" (Gen 13:10), irrigated by a river that split into four (Gen 2:10). It's the Bible's first reference to rivers and the first use of four, a number associated with universality—four corners of earth (Isa 11:12), four winds of heaven (Dan 7:2), four cornerstones of the temple (Ps 118:22). Genesis 2:10 is the first hint that Eden is not destination but source, the first suggestion that Adam is to be like water, extending the garden's fecundity beyond Eden. It's the Bible's first missionary text.

Rivers flow out with new life. But the sea is water of a different sort. Israel's enemies often come from the sea (Philistines, Sidonians), flooding Israel like the wave of a tsunami. Israel's heroes are landlubbers—shepherds, not sailors.[32] Israel has no Ulysses, Jason, or Aeneas. Its most famous sailor, Jonah, ends up overboard.[33] Even the lake of Galilee is too threatening to attempt a crossing.[34]

Channeled, fresh, living water gives life. Rivers make land fruitful, set boundaries between peoples, or join them as liquid roads. Rivers reconcile water with land to meet human needs. Every Israelite aspires to erect a little Eden, fruitful as a tree by a rippling stream (Ps 1:3; Num 24:6). Rivers are battle-scars, gifts from Yahweh, who "cleaved the earth with rivers" (Hab 3:9). When Yahweh strikes, springs spout from dry ground. With the thrust of his spear he open wounds in the earth like the wound of the last Adam, whose side pours out water and blood.

Civilizations arise on the shores of rivers, lakes, seas, or man-made reservoirs and aqueducts (Ps 24:1-2).[35] The Nile makes Egypt, and the Indus makes India. The Tigris and Euphrates form Mesopotamia—the land between the rivers—and the land of promise stretches from the River to the sea (Deut 11:24; Josh 1:4), with a river at the center, gladdening the city of God (Pss 36:7-10; 46:4). When Israel is obedient, prosperity flows like a river (Isa 48:18), and blessing softens the earth and soaks plowed ground (Ps 65:9–10). Land is founded on the sea, inhabited land on rivers. The Greek philosopher Thales was right: Water is at the base of everything! Baptism lays the foundation of a *new* world, the city and kingdom of God.

Yahweh is Lord of the water, the true storm God. In wrath, he sends drought (Lev 26:18–19; Deut 28:23–24) or throws hail like cannonballs (Exod 9:18–25; Rev 16:17–21). He destroys the first world with water (Gen 6–8) and inundates Egypt's river world with plagues of water, blood, and ice.

Israel longs for water from heaven. Judah is a wasteland "until the Spirit is poured out upon us from on high" (Isa 32:15). Yahweh promises "streams on the thirsty land," and in the next breath says, "I will pour out My Spirit on your offspring" (Isa 44:3). Israel looks for another Solomon who will be "rain upon the mown grass" (Ps 72:6).

Jesus is baptized to fulfill Yahweh's aquatic promises, to transform men filled with murk and mud into living water. From the beginning, Jesus lives in a new water world. He serves alongside Galilean fisherman (Matt 4:12–22). As Yahweh incarnate, Jesus strides the sea (Job 9:8; Pss 77:19; 107:23–30; Isa 43:19; Hab 3:16). So does Peter (Matt 14:22–33). He doesn't get far, but for a few moments he shares Jesus' mastery of the deep. What will happen when his faith grows? Acts tells the rest of the story. Paul can't stay off boats, and shipwrecks spice up his late-night yarns (Acts 27; 2 Cor 11:25). Israel's rivers gave them passage to other lands, but the sea is the whale-road to the four ends of the earth.

B ecause it is water, baptism says "new creation." It preaches the reconciliation of heaven and earth.[36] In baptism, we pass through the firmament sea to join a heavenly chorus (Rev 15:2–4). "When you renounce Satan," Cyril of Jerusalem told his catechumens, "God's paradise opens before you."[37] Baptism signifies the fulfillment of Israel's mission, as it commissions ambassadors to the western horizon, where the sun takes its evening bath.[38] It orients the church to a future when the Lord will have tamed the raging sea into a crystal river (Rev 21:1; 22:1–5).

Sons of Adam, we are of earth. Jesus is the man from heaven, and baptism gives us a share of his heavenly life. Baptism falls as a shower from the sky. If fruitful, we receive a blessing from God. If a weed-infested garden, we are destined for burning (Heb 6:7–8). At the font, we die to the old creation and rise in the new. By baptism, second-century church father Tertullian says, man is "being restored to God, to the likeness of him who had been aforetime in God's image."[39] As God's Word and Wind sculpted creation from the deep, so the Spirit hovers over the font to shape new creatures. We are born again of water and the Spirit (John 3:5) in the regenerating bath of holy baptism (Titus 3:5).[40] We undergo a sea-change, transfigured to something rich and strange.

Baptism points to Jesus, who rose from the dead as the firstfruits of the age to come. As it points to Jesus, baptism tells the world, "Behold, a new creation has come!" To the baptized, it's performative speech, effecting what it declares: "Behold, *you are* a new creation!" As more and more are baptized, baptism forms the church as the locus of new-creation life in a dead world.

THEREBY PREFIGURING THIS BATH OF YOUR HOLY BAPTISM

IV

KILLING AND SAVING FLOOD

"Through the flood, according to your
righteous judgment, [You] condemned the
unfaithful world, and according to your great
mercy, saved faithful Noah, even eight persons."

aptism announces the good news. It's an effective
sign of new creation. Wherever and whenever a
baptism occurs, God declares the reality of new
creation and gives the baptized person a share in that reality.
Baptism makes the baptized a new creature.

That sounds impossible. How can baptism be a "washing of regeneration" (Titus 3:5)? How can a little water give
new life? What *kind* of new life does baptism give? The whole
Bible answers that question. Every biblical picture or type of

baptism—the flood, circumcision, the exodus, the purification rites of Leviticus, the entry into Canaan, the water wonders of kings and prophets—captures one dimension of what it means to be a new creature in Christ. In the last chapter, we looked at the whole gem and saw that baptism signifies new creation. In each of the following chapters, we'll take a closer look at one of the facets. In this chapter, we look at the flood. We become new creatures when we pass through the flood waters and enter the ark of a greater Noah.

Water is life. We are made of earth and become fruitful only if we're regularly irrigated. How astonishing, then, that the first time the Bible records rainfall, it kills rather than makes alive!

Genesis 1–6 recounts three falls. Adam eats forbidden fruit in the garden, Cain kills his brother Abel in the field, and the sons of God intermarry with the daughters of men in the world, producing vicious Nephilim. Because of these three falls, the whole earth is engulfed with violence, and Yahweh regrets making it in the first place (Gen 6:1–6). According to his righteous judgment, he condemns the unfaithful world by decreating it. He dissolves water world with an overabundance of water. The sea produced the first living souls. Now, waters of life become waters of death. The world reverts to its original condition, a deep "formless and void" (Gen 1:2). From water it came; to water it returns.

In the swirling storm, "God remembered Noah" (Gen 8:1). When Yahweh remembers, creation begins to take form again. Yahweh's wind (Hebrew, *ruach*) blows over the waters (Gen 8:1), hovering like the Spirit (Hebrew, *ruach*) over the deep (Gen 1:2). A dove flits above the sea, bearing the olive branch that signals peace and prefiguring the Spirit-dove who descends to Jesus.[41] When Yahweh remembers, rising waters drop, covered mountains reappear, and Noah, his family, and the animals emerge from the ark onto the peaks of Ararat.

The flood prefigures baptism (1 Pet 3:19–21).[42] The flood was what baptism now is. The comparison jars us. We expect the *thing* to be bigger, more impressive, than the symbol. Peter seems to invert our expectations. How are a few drops of water, or even a whopping baptismal tank, similar to a worldwide, world-destroying flood? It's as if a symphony by Gustav Mahler builds to a crescendo only to fade to a piccolo solo. It's like meeting an action movie star only to discover he's 4'9", scrawny, and a bit of a geek. How can reality be so much less than the shadow?

We are jarred by Peter's words because our view of baptism is shrunken. After listing the benefits of baptism, Luther asks, "How can water do such wonders?"[43] We grasp Peter's logic only when we share Luther's amazement at the awe-inspiring rites of initiation.[44] We must learn to see a flood in the font.

Baptism is flood-like partly because it marks a haven in the hurricane. It preserves the faithful in "the holy ark of Christendom, dry and safe."[45] Baptism is an adoption ceremony. The wood of Jesus' cross grows into a new ark,[46] and every baptized person joins the eightfold family of a new and greater Noah.[47] Outside the ark of the church, judgment looms, but those washed into the church—with its nautically ribbed ceiling—are delivered.[48] Through the saving flood of baptism, children of Adam become brothers and sisters of the last Adam who is "at the right hand of God" (1 Pet 3:22). We become members of one another, no longer adrift and alone.

Both the flood and baptism tell us about our sin. In the days of Noah, even God doesn't try to repair things. He extinguishes all flesh and turns the globe into a graveyard.[49] There's a message there: sinners need something more radical than reform. We "need to die."[50] That may sound heartlessly stern, but it's our only hope. In moments of desperate clarity, we want to end it all and start over. Baptism says we're right to seek death.

As the antitype of the flood, baptism indicates the right kind of death. Noah and his family are delivered from a world stalked by Titans where "every intent of the thoughts of [man's] heart was only evil continually" (Gen 6:1–5). Old loyalties, old temptations, old habits, and old associations and networks are washed away, and the eight members of Noah's family receive new life on the far side of death. One way or another, the flood kills. Those outside the ark drown. Those in the ark die to the world that then was. Baptism doesn't just tell us that we need to die. It kills, and so gives the gift of death.[51] Baptized into the ark, we don't die with the world, but to the world.

P eter says baptism doesn't wash dirt from the flesh but saves by the appeal of a good conscience (1 Pet 3:21). He's not talking about hygiene. Nor does Peter take back what he gives; he doesn't mean, "Baptism saves you, only not really."

Hebrews also uses the distinction between flesh and conscience. Under the law, an unclean person purified his flesh by a cleansing sacrifice, but Jesus' sacrifice cleanses the conscience (Heb 9:13–14). According to Peter, Christian baptism isn't like the lustrations of the law, whose power extended only to flesh. Baptism saves because it cleanses dead works from the conscience. In baptism, God says our guilty past doesn't control us. Baptism speaks God's word of forgiveness. Baptism has power to save because it joins us to Jesus' resurrection, which buries death and rises to eternal life.

God doesn't merely declare. He acts. As he washed away everything in Noah's past, so he rinses away whatever idols you have clung to, whatever evil you have done, whatever sins plague your conscience. You died, Paul says, when you were united to Christ's death. Now, then: *consider* yourself dead (Rom 6:8, 11). Believe what baptism tells you. Christians don't live toward death but from death. Death lies behind us, and we live our baptismal death every day, killing the world's lusts and lures. As it gives the gift of death, baptism gives the gift of an open future.

The world needs to die, too. Baptism is a warning to Nephilim of every age. Every time God baptizes, he declares that the world's days are numbered, calls kings to kiss the Son who reigns with a rod of iron, and points to the last day when the Risen One will judge all men everywhere. This had a specific application in the first century. Jesus prophesies that a catastrophe will inundate Israel during the lifetime of the apostles: the coming of the Son of Man will be "just like the days of Noah" (Matt 24:37–38). In the first century, baptism was a prophetic sign that the old world was about to be overwhelmed by a tide of Romans, who wouldn't leave one temple stone on another. Later, baptism warned persecuting Romans that their world, too, would one day be swamped by barbarians. We're sometimes tempted by the excitement outside the ark. When the world entices you, remember the lesson of baptism: the world is dying. Don't abandon the ark of the church and make a shipwreck of your faith.

Noah is a second Adam. Like Adam, he's the father of the human race. All creatures, including Noah, are again commanded to multiply and fill the earth (Gen 8:17; 9:7; see 1:22, 28). Noah has dominion over animals (Gen 9:2; see 1:28). Humanity was estranged from creation; the baptismal flood reunites them.

But Noah doesn't return to a pre-flood condition. He's an improved, postdiluvian man, "Adam 2.0." He offers the first whole burnt offering, which represents the animal's ascension to Yahweh (Gen 8:20–22).[52] Like the animal, Noah ascends higher than Adam. Adam ate green plants, but Noah eats animal flesh (Gen 9:3–4). Yahweh authorizes Noah to enforce capital punishment (Gen 9:5–6). Yahweh planted a garden for Adam; Noah plants his own vineyard and enjoys Sabbatical wine (Gen 9:20–21).[53] When Adam sinned, Yahweh pronounced judgment; when Ham sins, *Noah* curses (Gen 9:20–27). Yahweh hangs a water-bow in the sky to signify his covenant partnership with Noah.

Baptized Noah is more radiantly godlike than Adam was. He is a *resurrected* Adam, on the far side of death. As early Christian apologist Justin the Martyr points out, the eight persons signify the eighth day, "wherein Christ appeared when he rose from the dead, forever the first in power."[54] Baptized into Jesus' resurrection, we live in a new week, a new time, the age of our Lord. Baptism isn't merely rescue or restoration. It's glorification.

Can we see why Peter thinks the baptism is greater than the flood? After all, which is greater, water that sweeps away cities and farms or water that purges the conscience? Which is greater, a deluge that kills or a deluge that kills *and* makes alive? Which is greater, an ark that rescues from a flood or an ark that protects from death and the devil? Don't be deceived by the simplicity of baptism. It's as world altering as a global flood.[55] For which is greater, a gigantic ark of gopher wood, or a world-circling tower built on a supple foundation of baptismal water?[56]

AND THROUGH THE BAPTISM OF
YOUR DEAR CHILD,
OUR LORD JESUS CHRIST,
HAS SANCTIFIED AND
SET APART THE JORDAN
AND ALL WATER FOR A SAVING FLOOD,
AND AN AMPLE WASHING AWAY OF SINS

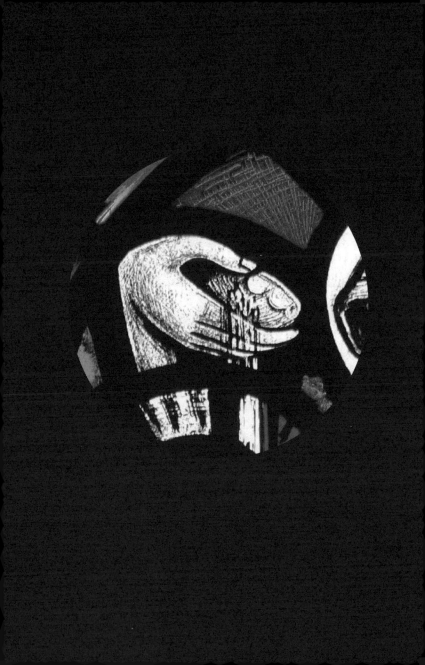

V

A CUT IN THE FLESH

"All that was born in him from Adam
... [is] drowned and submerged."

aptism proclaims the good news of a new creation. Baptism makes us new creatures by stripping off the flesh and giving the Spirit. To see how this works, we need to think about circumcision.

Noah lives in the tenth generation from Adam (Gen 5:3–32), and Abraham is born ten generations after Noah (Gen 11:10–26). Both Noah and Abraham are new Adams. In the early centuries of history, a new Adam arises every tenth generation.[57] Between Adam and Noah, the world becomes so evil that Yahweh regrets making man. He turns the world into a formless void, until his wind and word make dry land appear once again. In Noah, humanity gets a fresh start. Abraham also comes on the scene after wickedness has filled the earth. The men of Babel defy God (Gen 11:1–9). Instead of spreading out, they assemble on the plain of Shinar to build a city and a temple-tower to connect heaven and earth. Yahweh confuses their languages and scatters them over the face of the earth.

The world is ripe for judgment, but Yahweh doesn't send another torrent. Instead, he calls a single man from among the divided nations. He promises Abraham a land and seed to plant in it, a stream of descendants to carry God's blessing to the divided nations (Gen 12:1–3). As much as Noah, Abraham is a father of a new human race carved out from the old. Yahweh *commanded* Adam (Gen 1:28) and Noah (Gen 9:1) to be fruitful and multiply. He *promises* that Abraham's seed will fill the earth (Gen 17:6, 20).[58] Adam's vocation is narrowed down to one man, one family and nation, with God's guarantee it will be fulfilled.

As sign of the Abrahamic covenant (Gen 17:11), a literal cut in the flesh signifies the cut in humanity that separates Abraham's family from other families on earth. Separation isn't the goal. Adam's flesh was cut and his rib separated to make Eve (Gen 2:21–22), but he was divided for the sake of reunion: "the two shall become one flesh" (Gen 2:24). The cut in Abraham's flesh doesn't create a permanent rupture but looks toward the time when the two tributaries will flow together into One New Man (Eph 2:15), made one flesh in Jesus the bridegroom.

When Yahweh calls Abraham and Sarah from Ur, she's barren and he's old (Gen 11:30; 17:1), both as good as dead (Rom 4:19). Abraham is potent enough to father Ishmael (Gen 16), but the promise flows through Isaac, the miracle child of Abraham and Sarah (Gen 18:1–15; 21:1–7). Abraham hopes against hope, trusting the God who calls things that are not as though they were, the God who raises the dead (Rom 4:17–18). Coming from two dead parents, Isaac's birth is a resurrection.

Yahweh commands circumcision after Abraham fathers Ishmael but before Isaac is born. Circumcision removes foreskin from the penis. Abraham is already old, and Sarah is barren. Yahweh's startling solution is to instruct Abraham to wound his withered organ of generation. Circumcision is a symbolic castration, a repudiation of natural potency and a declaration of faith in God's power. *Yahweh* fathers his own family through Abraham and Sarah. Abraham's future doesn't depend on Abraham's power, but Yahweh's, who alone can give a son of the Spirit (Gal 4:29). How ironic that Pharisaical Jews in Paul's day turned this rite of renunciation of flesh into an occasion for boasting in the flesh!

In Colossians 2:11–12, Paul refers to the "circumcision of Christ" and links it, somehow, to baptism. Some see a direct line from circumcision to baptism: circumcision was Israel's sign of covenant inclusion; baptism is the church's.[59] Proponents of infant baptism often use Colossians 2 as a proof that infants should be baptized, just as infant boys were circumcised into Israel.[60]

Infant circumcision does tell us something important about Israel: it didn't consist only of those who had chosen to be Israelites. Before they chose anything, Hebrew males became bearers of the promises and obligations of the covenant. Israel wasn't a religious club for the mature, a philosophical caste for a spiritual elite, or a voluntary society. It was a *people*. As the nucleus of a new human race, Abraham's family included all sorts and conditions of men—infants (Ishmael) and the aged (Abraham), as well as hundreds of men and boys in Abraham's household, many of them slaves acquired in Egypt (Gen 12:16; 14:14; 17:22–27).

As I noted in chapter 1, most debates about baptism are really debates about the church. The quarrel about infant baptism is one of those. The question is: Does Jesus gather the same sort of people as Yahweh, or is the church a quite different kind of religious community? Does Jesus establish a club for the religiously mature, a voluntary society for adults who have made a conscious choice to follow him, or a people? The New Testament is clear. Jesus establishes a new Israel, calling twelve apostles as new patriarchs. He breaks down the dividing wall, not to form a religious order, but to form "one new man" (Eph 2:11–22). Those who were not a people become the people of the living God (1 Pet 2:10). The church is a royal priesthood and a holy nation (1 Pet 2:9).[61] As a nation, the church includes all sorts, conditions, and ages of men and women. As with all nations, many become citizens long before they're aware that nations exist.

Let's come at this from another angle. The Spirit is the gift promised to Abraham (Gal 3:6–14). When the Spirit rains down at Pentecost, he unties the knot of Babel, inspiring languages that unite rather than divide (Acts 2:5–11). The church is the un-Babel, an international nation, a polyglot multiculture united in the Son by the Spirit. It's the nation-of-many-nations promised to Abraham, and baptism is the naturalization ceremony. If this is what the church *is*, it must include not only the strong and mature but the weak, young, and helpless. In baptism, as in circumcision, God places his name on infants, claiming them as his own before they know or choose it. He draws us in his love, and we love him because he first loved us.

T his *isn't* what Paul is talking about in Colossians 2. The "circumcision of Christ" (Col 2:11) isn't baptism, but a circumcision performed *on* Jesus.[62] The cross is the present-tense reality prefigured by the future-tense rite of circumcision.[63] By his death, Jesus fulfills what circumcision anticipated: flesh is cut away; all that comes from Adam is removed. By his resurrection, he begins new life in the Spirit. Those joined to *Jesus'* circumcision are "circumcised with a circumcision made without hands" (2:11). United to Jesus' death, our flesh is rolled away so we can walk in the Spirit.

Baptism unites us with Christ's circumcision (Col 2:12). This is why Paul can speak of Christians as the "true circumcision" (Phil 3:3) in contrast to unbelieving Jews, who, though circumcised in body, don't share in *the* circumcision of Christ. In baptism, our flesh is stripped away, like the garment removed in some baptismal liturgies.[64] Though we continue to live in the flesh, we live by the faith of the Son of God (Gal 2:20), watered by the Spirit who battles our flesh and produces his fruit in the ground of our lives (Gal 5:22–24).

"Flesh" isn't just "sinfulness" but refers to our natural associations and affinities. Flesh divides. In baptism, fleshly identities—national, ethnic, familial, educational, economic—are submerged. All the baptized wear the family name of "Father, Son, and Spirit," relativizing all other names—"American," "Smith," "Yale law grad." This is how baptism into the circumcision of Christ makes us new creatures: it gives us a new identity and a new name, not of the flesh but of the Spirit.

We who receive one baptism are one people. When we splinter into factions, we defy our baptism and profane the name we wear (1 Cor 1:10–17). Schism is the way of flesh. Sharing one baptism and one name, we must preserve the unity of the Spirit (Eph 4:1–6). Baptism makes us one and then calls us to be what we are: brothers who dwell together in unity, pleasant as "the dew of Hermon" (Ps 133:1–3).

WE PRAY THAT THROUGH
YOUR SAME INFINITE MERCY
YOU WOULD GRACIOUSLY LOOK DOWN
UPON THIS YOUR CHILD,
AND BLESS HER WITH
A RIGHT FAITH IN THE SPIRIT

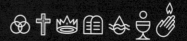

VI

DROWNING PHARAOH

"[You] have drowned hard-hearted Pharaoh
with all his army in the Red Sea, and have
led your people Israel dry through it."

fter a catena of Gospel texts about water, Tertullian
concludes, "Christ is never without water."[65]
What's true of the reality is true of the type, for
"Moses is never without water."[66]

Moses' life is full of water. Fearing the Hebrews' fecundity
in Goshen, Pharaoh drowns all male Hebrew infants in the
Nile (Exod 1:22). The Nile is a river of blood long before the
first plague (Exod 7:14–19). Israel has protectors. Mothers and
midwives guide infants through the death canal. In the womb
of his "ark,"[67] Moses passes through the Nile and rises to new
life in Pharaoh's house. His Egyptian name, *mosheh*, is a lifelong

reminder that he was "drawn out" of the waters (Exod 2:10).[68] Moses is a new Noah (Gen 5:29), an ancient example of infant baptism.[69]

What happens to the head, Moses, is recapitulated in the body, Israel. Yahweh "strengthens" Pharaoh's heart (Exod 4:21; 7:13, 22; 8:19; 9:12, 35)[70] so that he refuses to free Yahweh's son, Israel (Exod 4:22–23). So Yahweh takes Pharaoh's firstborn son at Passover: eye for eye, tooth for tooth, son for son. In a flourish of poetic justice, Yahweh drowns drowning Pharaoh in the Red Sea (Exod 14:28–31): eye for eye, tooth for tooth, water for water. Moses conquers the river of death, so he can lead Israel through the sea of death. Once midwifed through the Nile, Moses plays midwife at Israel's birth. All Israel is baptized into *mosheh*—Moses, the drawn-out one. They become a people drawn out.

I n the new exodus of baptism, "the gentiles ... leave behind, drowned in the water, their ancient tyrant the devil."[71] Some early writers imagine the devil as Pharaoh, chasing catechumens into the font, remembering too late that spirits can't swim.[72] As the sea killed Israel's enemy, so baptism destroys our own enmity to God, while we rise from the water "alive from the dead."[73] Liberation from Satan was ritualized in pre-baptismal exorcisms and renunciation ceremonies, where candidates renounced the devil, his works, his servants, and his pomp.[74] *We* are often Satanic accusers and tyrants. Baptism makes us new creatures by freeing us from ourselves and from a world under Satan's cruel domination. God gives new life among the people of the crucified and risen Lord.

After the exodus, Moses' sister Miriam leads Israel's women in a victory song (Exod 15:1–18). To Zeno of Verona, Miriam represents the church, who "leads the Christian people not into the desert but into heaven, singing hymns and beating her breast."[75] On the far side of baptism, we sing Miriam's taunt song: Yahweh is a warrior. He has thrown the horse and its rider into the sea.

As Alexander Schmemann notes, we moderns feel no need to renounce Satan because we "do not see the presence and action of Satan in the world." The world looks so shiny and civilized that we don't grasp how "such seemingly positive and even Christian notions as 'freedom' and 'liberation,' 'love,' 'happiness,' 'success,' 'achievement,' 'growth,' 'self-fulfillment' … can in fact be deviated from their real significance and become vehicles of the 'demonic.'" Baptism renounces "an entire 'worldview' made up of pride and self-affirmation" that twists life "into darkness, death and hell."[76] What appears to be a gentle, middle-class neighborhood can be a nest of vipers. Baptism enlists us to resist domesticated dragons as much as the feral ones.

We trivialize the devil, but we're haunted by ghouls of oppression and ghosts of victimization. Millions are scarred by sexual abuse or domestic violence. Hundreds of thousands stumble through nightmarish post-trauma from war, torture, genocide. Even materialists speak of "personal demons." To all such, baptism is gospel. Victimizers are rescued from their own cruelty, as the waters open a horizon of reparation and redemption. Baptism doesn't promise a trouble-free life. Israel was tempted in the wilderness, and Jesus faces off with Satan *after* his baptism (Matt 3:13–4:11).[77] Baptism begins a war with Satan. But baptism promises the oppressed a defender greater than Moses, a defender who is already Victor.

At an Eden-like well in Midian, Moses defends seven sisters from surly shepherds and draws water for them (Exod 2:16–17). Drawn from the water, Moses draws water. It's another head-and-body episode. After Israel passes through the Sea, Moses provides water for all Israel (Exod 17:5), and at Marah he sweetens brackish water by throwing wood into the pool (Exod 15:22–25).[78] In baptism, the watered become sources of water; those born of Spirit become springs of Spirit.[79] "Out of his innermost being will flow rivers of living water," Jesus said, and John adds, "But this he spoke of the Spirit" (John 7:38–39). The baptized are *mosheh*, drawn from death water to overflow with living water. Our baptismal exodus isn't merely freedom-from. It's freedom-for.

For Paul, the exodus is a warning (1 Cor 10:1–2).[80] *All* were delivered and *all* started a new life in the wilderness, yet "with most of them God was not well-pleased" (1 Cor 10:5). They grumbled and "were laid low in the wilderness" (1 Cor 10:5), "destroyed by the destroyer" (1 Cor 10:10). *This* is the type for us (1 Cor 10:6[81]). We're rescued from the devil to eat the bread of heaven and drink from the Rock. But after baptism we enter the wilderness. Water and bread don't guarantee we'll get to the promised land.

Paul raises the controverted question of the relation of baptism to faith. For Baptists, repentance and faith must precede the sign. For some proponents of infant baptism, faith arrives long after baptism, while for others baptism "creates" faith in infants.

We need to clarify what the Bible means by "repentance" and "faith." Even for adults, repentance doesn't precede baptism; baptism *is* repentance, the "turn" from Satan to Christ. "Repent *by being* baptized," Peter urges at Pentecost.[82] Repentance *always* follows baptism, since baptism begins a life of continuous repentance, such that "the Christian life," Luther says, "is nothing other than a perpetual baptism."[83]

Christian faith is loyalty to King Jesus.[84] In baptism, adults and infants are pledged to Jesus, sealed by the Spirit as soldiers, slaves, and sheep of God's pasture. The gift of baptism awakens faith, loyal allegiance to the one whose name we bear. If faith is loyalty, by definition it persists through thick and thin. A soldier who shrinks from battle isn't keeping faith with his commander. The Spirit gives the gift of faith and keeps us in faith; he keeps us loyal to our commander. What's crucial is not the size of our faith before baptism but the Spirit's gift of persevering faith after.

We need to take both sides of Paul's warning with full seriousness. All passed under the cloud, all were baptized into Moses, all ate and drank. All of that happened to every Israelite.

Yet many grumbled and fell. They were joined to Moses, then cut off. Adopted into Yahweh's family, they went prodigal. This happens to baptized Christians, too. Like sheep, they wander. Rescued from the devil, some surrender to him again and become noxious swamps. The existence of such people is a deep mystery. Why would a child betray a perfect Father? What makes an organ rebel against its own body? These traitors are like the ruthless steward in Jesus' parable, on whom the king reimposes an unpayable debt (Matt 18:23–43).[85]

Paul's warning provokes fear, but not despair. Godly fear goads us to endure in the faith of baptism. Remember Lot's wife, who died when she looked back wistfully to Sodom.[86] Kill your ingratitude before it kills you. Resist the lusts of the flesh and eyes, the pride of life. Forget the Egypt behind and stretch toward the glory ahead. Trust what God has declared about you in baptism. Keep the faith. In baptism, we're pledged to God's side. Relying on the Spirit, faith *stays* on his side.[87]

SO THAT
THROUGH THIS SAVING FLOOD
ALL THAT WAS BORN IN HER
FROM ADAM AND
ALL WHICH SHE HAS ADDED THERETO
MIGHT BE DROWNED AND SUBMERGED

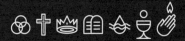

VII

AN AMPLE WASHING

"Sanctified ... all water ... [as] an
ample washing away of sins."

aptism is the effective sign of new creation. It
announces to the world that Jesus has inaugurated
new creation. It gives the baptized a share in that
new creation and remakes creation. As a new creature, the
baptized is rescued from the world and brought into the ark;
his flesh is stripped away so he can walk in the Spirit; he is
delivered from the devil to follow a new Moses.

Jesus the last Adam fulfills the vocation of humanity. As
a new man in the Spirit, Jesus is priest, conquering king, and
prophet. By baptism, we share his vocation. We are ordained
as priests, anointed as kings, inspired as prophets. Over the
next few chapters, we will look at each of these facets of new

creation in turn as we move from Leviticus to Joshua to the monarchy to the prophets.

B aptism is the bridal bath that prepares us for the marriage supper of the Lamb (Eph 5:25–26; Rev 19:9–10). This was true for Israel as for the church. To feast at the king's house, Israel needs to be pure. Many things pollute: eating unclean food (Lev 11), childbirth (Lev 12), skin disease (Lev 13), male genital discharges (Lev 15:1–17), sexual intercourse (Lev 15:18), menstruation (Lev 15:29–30), contact with a corpse (Num 19:1–22). Impurity isn't sin. A married couple is supposed to have sex, yet they're polluted by it (Lev 15:18). A man rightly honors his dead father, but attending the funeral makes him unclean for a week. After Adam, death, sin, and flesh reign (Rom 5:12–21). The rules of uncleanness symbolize the curse invading and infecting human life.

Impure people are excluded from Yahweh's house and table. To return, they have to perform rites of purification, most of which involve water "baptisms" (Heb 9:10). Touch or eat unclean meat, and you'll have to wash your body, launder your clothes, and wait to be cleansed by the evening sacrifice (Lev 11:24–28, 40). Once her monthly period ends, a woman washes her body and offers a sacrifice of birds (Lev 15:25–30). The cleansing agent for corpse defilement is the "water of purification," concocted from water and ashes from a burnt red heifer (Num 19:1–22).

Ablutions restore unclean Israelites to the tabernacle, the place of worship. Washing restores them to the liturgical community assembled at Yahweh's house. Like parents everywhere, Yahweh makes his children wash up before they come to the table.

At the tabernacle, Israel offers animal sacrifices, but sacrifice is more than slaughter, dismemberment, and burning (Lev 1–7). Yahweh erects his tent so Israel can feast with him (Deut 12:1–14). His is a royal house, and even palace courtiers have only limited access to the king's inner chambers. Yet the tabernacle's purpose is to be Yahweh's hall of hospitality.[88]

The main new offering at Sinai is the peace offering, the only sacrifice that common Israelites are permitted to eat (Lev 7:11–18). The sin (Lev 4) and trespass offerings (Lev 5:14–6:7), also introduced at Sinai, cleanse sin and compensate for offenses *so that* Israel can eat and drink with Yahweh. Priests offer "ascensions" *so that* they might climb the mountain to Yahweh's table. Israelites are Yahweh's "companions," those who share his bread (Lev 21:6, 8, 17, 21–22). At the trysting tent, Yahweh enjoys a continuous marriage supper with his bride, his "garden spring" (Song 4:12, 15) and his "fountain" (Prov 5:18).

Jesus' blood cleanses us through baptismal water. As we saw in the first chapter, baptism has this power because it unites us to Christ, who is pure and holy. In baptism, we join the company of the clean as members of the whole Christ that is the church. Baptism is more powerful than Israel's purifications.

In the Mosaic covenant, Israel had to wash repeatedly. In the new, we receive one baptism and we're welcome in God's house forever. Jesus bore the curse on the tree, ending the reign of death (Rom 5:12–21). Cleansed by baptism, we no longer live in fear of impurity. To the clean, all things are clean (Rom 14:20).

Baptism gives us a seat at the table of Jesus. Baptists have always known this: as soon as a convert is wet, he's admitted to the Eucharist. Many who baptize infants leave them in limbo, baptized but not yet table companions of Jesus. That's a doctrinal and practical error. If children are in the family, they eat the family meal. Once a child has washed up, why keep him away from dinner?[89]

We don't observe purity rites, yet we still experience shame and sense our pollution.[90] The obese man who recoils at his own body, the addict disgusted at the pathetic weakness of his will, the woman who can't see her pretty face in the mirror because her mother has always railed at her ugliness: all feel unclean. Shame, said John Paul II, is a withdrawal from visibility, "fear in the presence of a second I." When ashamed, we don't feel we have a right to visibility, so we erect screens between ourselves and others, between ourselves and God.[91] We're alien to the world itself; we feel unworthy to step out into God's cosmic temple.

To those who feel ashamed and unclean, baptism is gospel. Reborn by water and Spirit, the baptized shine with the dazzling light of God's beauty. Baptism dissolves the barriers of shame that screen us from God and one another. It makes us one flesh with the body of the whole Christ. Baptism harmonizes us with creation. In ancient rites, candidates were baptized naked because they were returning to innocent Eden, where Adam and Eve were "naked and not ashamed."[92]

B aptism also fulfills Levitical rituals of sanctification. Holiness and purity aren't the same. A clean person is permitted to enter the court of Yahweh's house and eat his food. When Yahweh occupies the Most Holy Place, he consecrates the entire tabernacle by his glory (Exod 29:43). Everything in the tent is holy, which means everything is his. Only holy persons may touch holy vessels and furnishings, tread on holy ground, and eat holy food. "Holy things for holy people" is the Levitical rule.

Every Israelite is a member of the "royal priesthood" and a citizen of the "holy nation" (Exod 19:6), but the priests possess a higher degree of holiness. To become a holy one—a saint— Aaron undergoes an elaborate ordination rite, known as the rite of "filling the hand" (Exod 29; Lev 8–9). At the beginning, Moses washes, anoints, and robes his brother. Many Christian writers see these rituals as shadows of the ample bath of holy baptism. As fourth-century theologian Ephrem the Syrian put it, "The oil is the dear friend of the Holy Spirit, it serves him, following it like a disciple. With it the Spirit signed priests and anointed kings."[93] Baptism sanctifies, anoints us with the *Holy Spirit*,[94] and clothes us as saints (Gal 3:27–28). We come from the font clean. We also come out sacred.

That means we are baptized to be living stones in God's holy house, the temple (1 Pet 2:4–5).[95] To know what this means, we need to learn more about Israel's sanctuaries. The tabernacle is a portable Sinai, a holy mountain in tent form.[96] Sinai is divided into three areas: Israel gathers at the base (Exod 19:17), the priests and elders ascend partway (Exod 24:9–11), and Moses enters the fiery storm cloud at the peak. Similarly, the tabernacle is divided into court, Holy Place, and Most Holy Place. Every Israelite enters the court, but only priests move through the firmament screen into the Holy Place, and only the high priest, a permanent Moses, enters the veil into the Most Holy Place, where Yahweh is enthroned on wings of golden cherubim. The tabernacle's zones portray status divisions within Israel, a sign that the sanctuary, and later Solomon's temple, represents a living temple, the people of Israel (John 2:19–21; 1 Cor 3:16–17; 6:19; Eph 2:21).

The tabernacle's curtains are interwoven with cherubim, a reference to Eden (Gen 3:22–24). Like Eden, Israel's sanctuaries are well-watered places (1 Kgs 7:23–39; Ezek 47:1–12). When demons take over God's house, its waters turn lethal (Rev 8:10–11). Between Adam and exodus, Yahweh had no fixed earthly address and no one entered his oasis. At Sinai, Aaron is ordained a new Adam, with his sons as helpers to tend God's new garden (Exod 29; Lev 8–9).[97]

The tabernacle is also a replica of the cosmic temple of creation. The court is earth with its altar-mountain. The Holy Place is the firmament, complete with seven stars on the menorah and the bread of heaven stacked on the golden table. The Most Holy Place, Yahweh's earthly throne room, mirrors heaven. If we're baptized into the house, we're restored to a proper relation to creation.

Baptism places us as the bricks and mortar in the temple of the Spirit. Luther speaks of baptism and the Lord's Table as "trysting places," designated locations where the Divine Lover loves his bride.[98] Baptism is a ritual clock. Like the word, like the Lord's Table, baptism is also a ritual map, the X that indicates the place of God's presence, where he distributes his gifts. Wherever baptism happens, the Lord says, "Seek me *here. Here* I can be found."[99] Each of us is a temple of the Spirit that is part of the universal temple. God seals us with his name and says of *us*, "Here I may be found."

Jesus is the Holy One, the high priest of the new covenant. By uniting us to Jesus' baptism, our baptism announces and forms a new order of sanctity. Every baptized person is a saint, a holy person, a priest.[100] Men *and women* are consecrated into the Christian priesthood. Freemen *and slaves* are clothed with Christ. Jews *and gentiles* are anointed by the one Spirit. Baptism makes a new priesthood. Every baptism adds another priest to the order.

We're not merely consecrated ones, but also consecrat*ing* ones, who sanctify everything and everyone by the word of God, prayer, and thanksgiving (1 Tim 4:4). We don't act as priests only in worship or at church. In our daily work, in our families, and among our friends, we set apart all things to God with lives of continuous thanks.

Now the people *are* the temple, and our priestly ministry is transformed as a result. Priests guard God's house, and the baptized guard one another from the contamination of sin. Priests offer incense, and we intercede for one another. Priests bring sacrifices to the altar, and baptism forms a choir offering a sacrifice of praise. Priests replenish the oil and trim the wicks of the lampstand. We seek a continuous supply of the Spirit so our light will shine before men; we trim and replenish one another so the whole church blazes like a city of light on a hill.

The priestly ordination rite is called "filling the hand." Baptism fills *our* hands with gifts and a mission. The baptized have their hands full.

AND THAT SHE MAY BE SEPARATED FROM THE UNFAITHFUL

VIII

CROSSING JORDAN

"[God] has sanctified and set apart the
Jordan and all water for a saving flood."

 aptism makes us new creatures by making us
priests. It also makes us new creatures by making
us conquerors, soldiers of Jesus, the new and
better Joshua.

Water is a boundary. When Israel leaves Egypt, they surge
out through the Red Sea and into the wilderness. Yahweh makes
the arid land a fertile field and rains bread from heaven, but the
wilderness isn't a permanent home. To flourish, Israel needs to
flow *into* Canaan.

When they do, they again cross a water boundary. Yahweh
uncovers dry ground, as he did on the third day of creation (Gen
1:9–10) and at the Red Sea (Exod 14:16, 21). He heaps up the
water of the Jordan—during flood season no less (Josh 3:14–17).

As Israel is baptized into Moses, so they are baptized into Joshua, whose miracles mark him as a new Moses.[101] Unlike the Red Sea, the Jordan doesn't kill. No world is wiped away. No Pharaoh drowns. The Jordan is a river of life.[102] To enter the land, Israel needs both a baptism through death and a baptism of resurrection.

When Israel enters Canaan, Yahweh begins to fulfill the promise to Abram (Gen 15:17–21). Following Joshua, Israel claims a land of milk and honey, a land moistened by the rain of heaven, a land of cities, vineyards, and orchards they neither planted nor built (Deut 6:10–11; Josh 12–21). Baptism in the Jordan is an effective sign of their inheritance—a sign because it symbolizes the promise, effective because it grants their birthright.

Israel marches from Egypt to Moab, east of the Jordan (Num 22:1; Deut 34:1–8). Entering the land, they move east to west. That axis is noteworthy. Yahweh set cherubim at the eastern gate of Eden to block westward reentry (Gen 3:24). A priest moves westward to enter Yahweh's throne room (Exod 26:22, 27). Crossing the Jordan from east to west, Israel is a new humanity, restored to an Eden that has expanded to become a garden land. They're baptized in the Jordan as a priestly people, entering sacred territory, the holy land.

Before Israel settles, they fight. Baptizing Israel into Joshua, Yahweh musters his conquering host. Passing through the flood, Israel *becomes* a flood that inundates Canaan to sweep away idols, idolaters, and their shrines.[103] Though battles lie ahead, baptism ensures their ultimate victory. Yahweh the divine warrior leads, so Israel fights with utter confidence about the final outcome. This is why Joshua employs such peculiar tactics. Israel demolishes the walls of the great city, Jericho, with a priestly procession, a shout of acclamation, and trumpet fanfare (Josh 6). Whenever Israel is victorious, Yahweh is the hero.

The new covenant begins at the same river, where John the Baptist preaches a baptism of repentance. Rome has already laid its axe at the dry roots of Israel and will chop and burn unless Israel repents (Matt 3:1–10). John drenches a remnant so they can bear the fruit of repentance and escape the fire.

John deliberately chooses to baptize in the wilderness of the Jordan (Matt 3:6).[104] Because of Israel's sins, Yahweh delivered his people into exile. Though they returned to the land, they are fruitless because they are not well planted, well tended, or well watered. Pouring water in the wilderness, John dramatizes the coming exodus and conquest.[105] Heavenly rain will turn the wilderness into a pool of water, and a new Israel, baptized with his Jordan baptism, will inherit the land.

Jesus is a new Joshua. Cyril of Jerusalem highlights many similarities. After passing through the Jordan, Joshua "began to rule over the people," while Jesus "began to preach the gospel." Jesus calls twelve apostles as Joshua "appointed twelve tribes to divide the inheritance." The figurative Joshua "saved Rahab the harlot," and the true Joshua welcomes "publicans and harlots ... into the kingdom of God." Joshua fought at Jericho, while Jesus prophesies the destruction of Jerusalem: "With only a shout the walls of Jericho fell down. ... And because Jesus said, 'There shall not be left here one stone upon another,' the Temple of the Jews opposite to us is fallen, the cause of its fall not being the denunciation but the sin of the transgressors."[106]

As the new Joshua, Jesus conquers and inherits all nations (Ps 2). Baptized into his Jordan baptism, we're co-conquerors and co-heirs, planted in the heavenly land that is Jesus, the Zion that is the whole Christ.[107] As Jesus receives the Spirit at baptism, so we receive the Spirit who will one day free creation from vanity (Rom 8:12–25) as a down payment on our future inheritance (2 Cor 1:22; 5:5; Eph 1:13–14).[108] Even now, we taste the future.

F or some Christians, talk of conquest and inheritance feels alien or even immoral. Ancient Israel conquered territory, but Christians are called to suffer in and with Jesus, a suffering servant rather than a conquering commander. Ancient Israelites inherited earth, but we Christians look for a heavenly country.[109]

We must resist these spiritualizing tendencies. We are of the faith of Abraham and so are heirs with Abraham, who is "heir of the *world*" (Rom 4:13). All things belong to those who are in Christ, whether life or death or things present or things to come or heaven or earth. Everything is ours because we are Christ's and Christ is God's (1 Cor 3:18–23). Creation, this creation *and* the next, belong to the baptized. Like Achsah, Caleb's daughter, who asks her father for the springs of water as her dowry (Josh 15:18–19), the church asks our Father for this world and the well-watered world to come as our inheritance.

It's ours, and we have the technology to conquer it. Baptism enlists us in the great war of human history, among the troops of the seed of the woman as he fights the seed of the serpent. As it brings us into the army of the church, baptism equips us with a panoply of weapons—the belt of truth, the breastplate of righteousness, the sandals of the gospel of peace, the shield of faith, the helmet of salvation, and the sword of the Spirit, which is the word of God (Eph 6:12–17). The warfare of the baptized is a warfare of faith fought with Spiritual weapons (2 Cor 10:1–6), a liturgical warfare of word, water, song, prayer, bread, and wine.[110] We're deployed to demolish idols and every rival to Jesus, wherever they appear—in our own hearts,[111] in the church, at work, in the world around us. Baptism calls us to resist every tyrant, petty or potent, in the name of Jesus. We're certain our Commander will conquer and reign until all his enemies are beneath his feet (1 Cor 15:25). Baptism makes us new creatures in Christ by placing us on the winning side.

Because we're heirs of God, all things serve us.[112] Sickness offers a chance to bear a cross with good cheer. Poverty serves our maturation. Wealth is an opportunity for generosity. Because all things are ours, wealth belongs to the poor and poverty serves the wealthy. Death is an enemy, but we own death, too. We learn to love this enemy, as death becomes a passage into the presence of the Lord. All the micro-deaths we suffer are enemies, but we love them for the new life they bring. Nothing, nothing, *nothing* exists but that it serves our good. Baptism unites us to Jesus, the Lord who became servant of all. The baptized man or woman is, Luther says, "perfectly free lord of all," while being "subject to all."[113]

AND PRESERVED IN
THE HOLY ARK OF CHRISTENDOM
DRY AND SAFE

IX

RAIN ON MOWN GRASS

"Bless her with a right faith in the Spirit."

When Jesus is baptized, the Spirit descends as a dove and rests on him (Matt 3:16; Luke 3:22; John 1:32). At Pentecost, Peter urges his hearers to be baptized to receive a share of the Spirit poured out on the apostles (Acts 2:38). The Spirit baptizes us into one body, harmonizing Jew and gentile, slave and free, male and female (1 Cor 12:12–13). Jesus tells Nicodemus, "Unless one is born of water and the Spirit, he cannot enter the kingdom of heaven" (John 3:5).[114] Like the first creation (Gen 1:2), Jesus, who embodies the new creation, emerges from the water by the energy of the Spirit.[115] So do we.

The Spirit is the oil that anoints Jesus as the Light of the World and equips him as servant to preach good news to the poor, release captives, give sight the blind, free the oppressed

(Isa 11:1–9; Luke 4:16–21).[116] The Spirit anoints us, too. In some Christian traditions, initiation includes anointings before and after water baptism.[117] Whether or not oil is used, the baptized *are* anointed, incorporated into the body anointed with the Spirit. In the Anointed One, we're anointed ones, "christs" in the Christ (1 John 2:20). We're filled with the oil of the Spirit to shine with good works, empowered by the Spirit to continue the work of the Servant.[118] Like judges, we become the Spirit's berserkers (Judg 3:10; 6:34; 11:29; 13:25; 14:6, 19; 15:14). Like Bezalel and Oholiab, we receive wisdom from the Spirit to build and adorn God's house (Exod 31:2–3; 35:30–31). Every baptism is a little Pentecost, as the Spirit rushes in with wind and fire.

In Israel, the chief "anointed ones" were priests, kings, and prophets. Saul, David, and Solomon are anointed into kingship (1 Sam 9:16; 10:1; 16:1–13; 1 Kgs 1:34, 38–40), and all receive the Spirit to carry out their royal mission (1 Sam 10:1–13; 16:13; 1 Kgs 3:1–14; see also Deut 34:9; Isa 11:1–2). Elijah anoints Elisha to succeed him as prophet (1 Kgs 19:16), and at Elijah's departure, Elisha receives a double portion of Elijah's spirit (see ch. 10). As anointing, baptism forms a communion of kings and prophets. In this chapter we'll think about baptism and kingship; in the next chapter, we'll consider what it means to be part of a company of prophets.

Justice is the hallmark of biblical kingship, and the baptized are anointed as justice warriors, like the king of Psalm 72 (see also Isa 32:1–2). The king gives justice because he receives the gift of justice (Ps 72:1). Under his reign, justice ripples from the mountain of the king's palace—the mountain that is the king himself—bringing peace to the land below. Just kings are water, ruling with wisdom deep as the sea (Prov 18:4). Just kings speak and enforce God's words and judgments. The king's name endures because it's incorporated into the name of Yahweh, blessed forevermore (Ps 72:2–3).

Care of the poor, vulnerable, weak, destitute, and isolated is *the* biblical standard of a just society. No society is just or healthy if the weakest aren't protected, if you need money to get a fair hearing in a court, or if the poor are denied opportunities to flourish. The king's justice especially blesses the needy and poor (Ps 72:4, 12–14). He passes judgment in their favor and saves the helpless by crushing their oppressors, as Yahweh crushed the head of Rahab, the Egyptian sea monster (Isa 51:9).

The king's justice is summed up by the lovely phrase: "The king is like rain upon the mowing, like showers that water the earth" (Ps 72:6; my translation). Without the rain of justice, *everything* dies—the garden withers to a wasteland. When a just king reigns, grain stalks stand tall and spread like cedars of Lebanon, and cities flourish like green fields, fresh as Eden (Ps 72:16).[119] Rain refreshes and cleanses, glorifies and brightens. Rain on the mowing promises a future harvest beyond today's harvest. Blessed by Yahweh, the just king baptizes the land. Justice rolls down like waters, righteousness like an ever-flowing stream (Amos 5:24). A good shepherd, the king leads his people to refreshing springs (Ps 23:2; Isa 49:10). When the king gives Sabbath relief, the land becomes "a spring of water, whose waters do not fail" (Isa 58:11). The Lord directs the channel of the king's heart, to irrigate or flood (Prov 21:1).

Like all the Psalms, Psalm 72 is about Jesus. In Psalm 72, we pray that Jesus would reign so that rulers bring tribute and prostrate themselves before him. We pray that Jesus would deliver the needy and crush oppressors. We pray that Jesus would form his just society. Jesus fulfills his royal vocation primarily by his faithful witness to truth and his kingly self-gift for his people. The cross is his throne, and justice runs down from the mount called Golgotha.

Baptism is the good news that Jesus' royal rain has fallen from heaven to earth, and it incorporates the baptized into Jesus' work. Jesus establishes his justice through his body. United with the King, we're kings and queens, new Adams and Eves. By baptism, we dissonant children of Adam begin to resonate with creation. Soaked with heavenly rain, we become refreshing water for the world. The church is a cascade that sweeps away brutes and thugs; the church is a gentle shower to revive the thirsty and a cooling cup of mercy and justice, offered in compassion and humility. Whatever is born of flesh is flesh; what is born of Spirit is Spirit. Born of word, we are God's word to the world. Born of water, we are water.

Paul explicitly links baptism with justice. Dead and buried with Jesus in baptism, we share in his resurrection. Even *now*, we live resurrection life *in the body*. Sin no longer reigns over us, and so we don't need to devote our bodies to injustice (*adikia*). Baptism frees us to present the organs of our baptized bodies as instruments of the justice (*dikaiosune*) of God (Rom 6:1–14). Our baptized eyes discern good and evil. Our ears are open to truth. Our feet walk in righteousness, and our hands wield weapons of justice. Justified from sin by union with Christ's death (Rom 6:7), we become citizens of the just society that flows through the desert of human society, called to bend the arc of history toward God's justice.

In the just society of the baptized, the weak aren't simply *recipients* of care. They receive special honor because they, like every member of the body, have Spiritual gifts for the common good (1 Cor 12:14–26).[120] The strong don't dominate. We often think of power as the ability to bend others to our will or as the force to curb or suppress bad behavior. Those can be legitimate exercises of power, but power is fundamentally *empowerment*. We exercise power by granting power. As parents, employers, church leaders, political rulers, in whatever sphere we exercise power, we're rain on the mowing, showers to water the earth.

We seek justice as Jesus did, by witnessing to truth. We share his cruciform throne and reign as we offer ourselves as martyrs.[121] Daily life affords many opportunities for the quiet witness of generosity, kindness, evangelism. Daily life affords plenty of opportunities for bold witness—protesting when our employer abuses employees or cooks the books, resisting when our company donates to a wicked cause or starts an ad campaign that celebrates perversity, speaking the name of Jesus when we're told to shut up. Every baptism is a baptism into blood.

Kings are builders. Bezalel of the royal tribe of Judah is the craftsman who makes the furnishings of the tabernacle (Exod 31:2–3). Solomon son of David builds the first temple. Paul portrays himself as a new Bezalel, a "wise master builder," whom the Spirit equips to edify the house of God (1 Cor 3:517). Jesus is chief architect and builder, but, baptized into his royal office and action, we are co-builders. As a royal anointing, baptism confers not only a judge's sword, but a mason's trowel.

Sadly, the church has often joined the torturers, driven by lust for domination. At those times and places, we abandon our baptism. But baptism doesn't abandon us. Baptism is the Spirit's pledge to *remain* with us and to call us back when we wander.

David acts with brutal injustice when he commits adultery and murder. When Saul sinned, the grieved Spirit abandoned him (1 Sam 16:14). Saul's heart remained unbroken, but the price of wholeness was the loss of the Spirit of Yahweh. "Take not your Spirit from me" (Ps 51:11) means "Don't let me be a Saul." David wants the Spirit, even if he must pay with a broken heart. Heartbroken, David weeps and fasts, so he is sprinkled with hyssop and cleansed in his inner parts (Ps 51:7).

Baptism makes us kings. It calls us to fight with spiritual weapons of prayer, righteousness, faith, the sword-word of the Spirit. It commissions us to rule with wise justice and to build with skill. When we sin, baptism assures us that "the sacrifices of God are a broken spirit; a broken and a contrite heart, O God, You will not despise" (Ps 51:17). Baptism promises that the Spirit dwells among the fragments of a shattered heart.

AND MAY BE EVER FERVENT IN SPIRIT
AND JOYFUL IN HOPE
TO SERVE YOUR NAME,
SO THAT SHE WITH
ALL THE FAITHFUL MAY BE WORTHY
TO INHERIT YOUR PROMISE
OF ETERNAL LIFE,
THROUGH CHRIST JESUS OUR LORD.

X

SPIRIT OF PROPHECY

"Fervent in spirit and joyful in hope."

"This is what was spoken of through the prophet Joel," Peter announces at Pentecost (Acts 2:16). *What was spoken by the prophet Joel?* In the last days, God will pour out his Spirit indiscriminately on all flesh, not merely on Israel. As a result, "your sons and your daughters shall prophesy, and your young men shall see visions, and your old men shall dream dreams" (Acts 2:17–18). When the Spirit comes, he forms a community of prophets intoxicated with the Spirit, fulfilling Moses' wish that all the Lord's people would be prophets (Num 11:29). This is the good news of Pentecost: the Spirit makes us new creatures, that is, he makes us prophets.

Peter's hearers ask what they can do to wash away the guilt of crucifying the Lord of glory and join the merry band of prophets. Peter answers, "Repent, and each of you be baptized in the name of Jesus Christ for the forgiveness of your sins; and you will receive the gift of the Holy Spirit" (Acts 2:38). Repent by being baptized, and you'll get the eyes of a visionary, the mind of a dreamer, the tongue of a prophet. Old and young, male and female, Jew and gentile, slave and free—all the baptized share the Spirit (Gal 3:27–28).[122] No wonder some of the church fathers thought Pentecost, as well as Easter, a suitable time for baptism.[123]

Visions guide the early church's mission. Saul sees a vision on the road (Acts 26:19), and Ananias sees a vision telling him to find Saul (Acts 9:10). No visions, no Paul. Cornelius seeks out Peter because of a vision (Acts 10:3–6), and a vision prods Peter to visit Cornelius (Acts 10:9–17), where he witnesses a gentile Pentecost (Acts 10:44–48). No visions, no gentile mission. A vision impels Paul to sail the Aegean to Macedonia (Acts 16:9–10), and Agabus's prophecy warns Paul about his arrest in Jerusalem (Acts 21:11–14).

What about after Acts ends? Do our daughters *still* see visions and our old men dream dreams? Non-Pentecostals (like me) are liable to get spooked and run for cover. We shouldn't. Constantine saw a portent in the sky and began to worship the God of the Christians. The world has never been the same. Wasn't that a sign from the Spirit? Didn't the Spirit rouse William Carey and Hudson Taylor? Didn't the Spirit energize the prophetic words of John Paul II, which shattered an iron wall and broke the chains of millions? Hasn't the church always ridden in the wake of seers, dreamers, and wild-eyed prophets? Whatever we say about Pentecostalism and the charismatic movements, we must say this: the Spirit of Pentecost is with us still. The promise of Joel is still operative among the baptized.

Prophets are covenant attorneys, members of Yahweh's court.[124] Moses enters the cloud to speak with Yahweh mouth to mouth (Num 12:8), and Elijah flees to Horeb to present an indictment of Israel (1 Kgs 19:1–18). Micaiah enters Yahweh's council (1 Kgs 22:13–23), Isaiah sees Yahweh enthroned in glory, surrounded by seraphim (Isa 6:1–7), Ezekiel climbs aboard Yahweh's chariot (Ezek 1:1–28), and Daniel fasts and prays until an angel fills his mind with alarming visions (Dan 9:1–23). Yahweh ignites fires in prophets' mouths (Isa 6:6–7)—words to pluck up and plant, destroy and build (Jer 1:4–10). He feeds them scrolls (Ezek 3:1–11; Rev 10:1–11) so they become living words, for you are what you eat. Prophets hear Yahweh's judicial decrees and deliver them to the people. Prophets have the privilege of the floor to bring Israel's case before Yahweh (Amos 7:1–9). Prophets preach and intercede (Gen 20:7).

Prophets assume leading roles during the reign of Ahab of Israel. Elijah is a new Moses, and, like his predecessor, Elijah is never without water. Elijah summons a drought to curse Ahab's land (1 Kgs 17:1); as prophet, he controls the spigot of the sky (Jas 5:17–18). When Ahab and Jezebel attack him, he flees (1 Kgs 17:3), as Moses escaped from Goshen to Midian

(Exod 2:11–15). Like Israel, Elijah receives miracle bread and water in the wilderness. Both Elijah and Moses encounter women (Exod 2:16–22; 1 Kgs 17:8–16) associated with water: Moses provides water for the daughters of Jethro, and Elijah asks the widow of Zarephath for a drink.

When Elijah returns to the land, he performs more water wonders. Elijah's contest with the prophets of Baal is a contest of fire: which deity can light the sacrifice (1 Kgs 18)? Elijah makes it a contest of water by drenching his altar with four pitchers of water poured three times—a twelvefold torrent (1 Kgs 18:34–35). A Greek Epiphany prayer invokes the Triune God "who hast manifested to us in Elias the Thesbite, by the triple pouring of water."[125] Cappadocian father Gregory of Nyssa sees the combination of fire and water as the "sacramental rite of baptism," a sign that "where the mystic water is, there is the kindling, warm, and fiery Spirit, that burns up the ungodly, and illuminates the faithful."[126]

At the end of his ministry, Elijah again leaves the land, with Elisha doggedly following (2 Kgs 2). At the Jordan, Elijah rolls his cloak and cleaves the river with it, so the two prophets cross on dry land. Washed like an offering (Lev 1:9), Elijah is "better prepared" to ascend.[127] Passing west to east through the river, the two prophets reverse Israel's progress into the land, acting out a preview of Israel's later exile in Assyria and Babylon. Having defiled the land, Israel will descend into the deep of exile.

Elisha asks for a double portion of Elijah's spirit. A "double portion" is the inheritance of the firstborn (Deut 21:17), which Elisha expects from Elijah, his father (2 Kgs 2:12). As Elijah rises in the fiery whirlwind, Elisha watches and receives the spirit he asked for, signified by Elijah's mantle (2 Kgs 2:11–14). Elisha returns to the land, filled with Elijah's spirit and power. He repeats the Jordan baptism in reverse, a preview of his miracle-sodden ministry (2 Kgs 2:14). Elisha's baptism is a story of return as well as departure.

Elijah is a prophetic Moses, Elisha his Joshua. As Joshua was filled with the power of Moses, so Elisha carries on in the spirit of Elijah. He purifies fetid water with salt (2 Kgs 2:19–22). He predicts Yahweh will provide drinking water for Israel's dehydrated troops (2 Kgs 3:4–20), and the same water gives Israel victory (2 Kgs 3:21–27). He blinds an Aramean regiment and leads them to Samaria, then graciously sends them away with bread and water (2 Kgs 6:8–23). To retrieve an iron axe head, Elisha throws wood into the Jordan (2 Kgs 6:1–7).[128] Because the axe head is borrowed, the man who loses it may have to pay by going into debt slavery. By recovering the iron, Elisha redeems him from bondage. The axe head sinks, like Jonah or like David when flooded by enemies, and the floating axe is the sign of Jonah, a symbol of liberating resurrection.[129]

Naaman, a Aramean general seeking a cure for leprosy (2 Kgs 5), is initially contemptuous of Elisha's command to bathe in the Jordan; he doesn't understand "the great mystery of the Jordan."[130] He eventually dips in the river seven times, recalling the days of creation, and his skin becomes smooth as a newborn's. Naaman's baptism is a new birth that returns him to the womb of the Jordan.

L ike all covenants, the new covenant begins with prophets, John and Jesus (Matt 21:11; Luke 24:19), a new Elijah followed by a wonder-working Elisha. Together, they inaugurate a new era of prophets. The sequence from Elijah to Elisha also foreshadows the transition from Jesus to his disciples, from Christ to the whole Christ. When Jesus is swept to heaven, he pours out a double portion of his prophetic Spirit. Still today, he clothes us with the mantle of the Spirit, so we can carry on his prophetic mission. [131]

We're all Naaman, lepers reborn. We're all iron sinking toward Sheol until the wood and water save us. We're all Elijah, led to brooks in the wilderness. We're all Elisha, baptized into Jesus' Jordan baptism to share his Spirit. By the Spirit of Jesus, the baptized become a prophetic community, given the words of God to speak and sing to one another, qualified by the Spirit to stand in the Lord's council. Preachers aren't the only prophets in the church. Preachers lead and train a community of prophets. Wherever the Lord calls us to labor—whether we're at work, home, out in the neighborhood, or at the kids' baseball game—he fills our mouths with words of fire to kill and make alive (1 Sam 2:6; Jer 1:9–10).

Prophets must keep up a steady diet of God's word so that our words give life rather than spread death. When we drink the Spirit, our words drop like rain and drip like dew (Deut 32:2). Clothed with the Spirit of prophecy, we intercede for the world. Faithful prophets must be and remain filled with the Spirit. You're baptized: walk in step with the Spirit. You've been soaked in the Spirit: don't quench or grieve him, and you will prophesy, you will see visions, you will dream dreams.

AMEN.

EPILOGUE

To the Baptized

vangelists preach to nameless crowds. The Bible is full of promises, but none is addressed directly to you.

Baptism *is*. At your baptism, the minister spoke to you: "Sarah, Sam, Sadhil, Sidra, Sabir: I baptize *you* into the name of the Father, and of the Son, and of the Holy Spirit." God wove your name into his, as he welcomed you into the common life of Father and Son in the Spirit. That's who you are. Baptism is the gospel with *your name* on it.

The gospel is good news of new creation. By his resurrection, Jesus has entered fully into the life of the Spirit; by water and the Spirit, he brings us into new-creation life. In your baptism, God made the gospel real in your life. You're reborn by water and Spirit, translated from a dead world into the life of Christ's one body animated by the one Spirit. You're in the ark, safe with your family from the deluge. With Abraham, you're heir of the world. God drowned your demons at the font and drafted you into the army of a greater Joshua, deployed to crush idols, fight injustice, and battle every false Messiah. You're sanctified as priest to sanctify and offer living sacrifice, anointed as king, filled with the Spirit of prophecy. Your past no longer controls you, now or ever. In baptism, God made his future yours.

Baptism's power doesn't stop when the water dries. God preaches in your baptism every day. When the bullies and demons return, remind Jesus and yourself you are *his*. When you want to slink into the shadows, God says, "You are robed in Christ." When you feel shackled by your past, God calls you to the future he opened at the font. Whenever you're insulted or falsely accused, hear God's declaration: "Whoever has died [in baptism] is justified from sin" (Rom 6:7). When you're fearful, call on the Spirit, and he will give you words to speak. When a murderous mob surrounds you, remember your baptism is fulfilled in martyrdom. You are what *God* says you are, not what you feel. Consider yourself to be who baptism says you are.

Whatever happens, you are in your Father's love. Trust him. Stay loyal. Don't "melt like water" (Josh 7:5). Plunged in God's water, you become God's water. Imitate the fish. Live in the water, and be God's rain on dry ground, God's flood against the wicked. Be God's water, for nothing is more powerful than water.

ACKNOWLEDGMENTS

I've been writing about and performing baptisms since I was ordained thirty years ago, and I'm grateful to Todd Hains and Jesse Myers for giving me the challenge of compressing what I've learned. This little book doesn't live up to my dreams for it (no book does), but it comes close due to the efforts of the Lexham Press team. Thanks too to Rev. John Barach for proofreading and indexing.

I finished the initial manuscript on May 29, 2020, the first anniversary of the death of my father, Dr. Paul Leithart, at the age of 98. He would have appreciated the Lutheran overtones of this book, and I wish I could have discussed it with him, long my most attentive and encouraging fan. I dedicate it to him in loving memory and gratitude for his lifelong example of faith in the Triune God who claimed him in baptism.

NOTES

1. The 1982 ecumenical statement *Baptism, Eucharist, and Ministry* (Geneva: World Council of Churches) claims a "large measure of agreement" (vii), but that convergence excludes large segments of the global church.

2. J. D. C. Fisher, *Christian Initiation: The Reformation Period* (London: SPCK, 1970), 11. See also Martin Luther, "The Order of Baptism Newly Revised" (1526), LW 53:107–8.

3. Gregory of Nyssa is a close competitor: "For you truly, O Lord, are the pure and eternal fount of goodness, who did justly turn away from us, and in loving kindness did have mercy upon us. You did hate, and were reconciled; you did curse, and did bless; you did banish us from Paradise, and did recall us; you did strip off the fig-tree leaves, an unseemly covering, and put upon us a costly garment; you did open the prison, and did release the condemned; you did sprinkle us with clean water, and cleanse us from our filthiness. No longer shall Adam be confounded when called by you, nor hide himself, convicted by his conscience, cowering in the thicket of Paradise. Nor shall the flaming sword encircle Paradise around, and make the entrance inaccessible to those that draw near; but all is turned to joy for us that were the heirs of sin: Paradise, yes, heaven itself may be trodden by man: and the creation, in the world and above the world, that once was at variance with itself, is knit together in friendship: and we men are made to join in the angels' song, offering the worship of their praise to God. For all these things then let us

sing to God that hymn of joy, . . . [as] the bride of Christ, who is, and was, and shall be, blessed now and for evermore. Amen" (in Thomas Finn, *Early Christian Baptism and the Catechumenate: West and East Syria* [Collegeville, MN: Liturgical Press, 1991], 82). Cyprian, third-century bishop of Carthage, says explicitly what's implicit in many writers: all water evokes baptism (*Epistle* 63.8.1).

4. I have worked out this point more fully in chapter 3 of *The Baptized Body* (Moscow, ID: Canon Press, 2007), entitled "The Body of Christ Is the Body of Christ."

5. Outside of quotations, I will mostly avoid the term "sacrament." First, some Christians reject the term as unbiblical, which, strictly speaking, it is. I don't reject the term, but I don't want anyone to stumble over my phrasing. Second, the word means many different things. It can refer narrowly to a handful of Christian rites; it can name an ontology. Rather than fill up space sorting through these different meanings, I avoid the term altogether.

6. *Answer to Faustus* 19. The medieval scholastic Thomas Aquinas quotes Augustine to explain the necessity of the sacraments (*Summa Theologiae* 3.61.1). For Thomas, the sacraments are necessary because the church is necessary. Augustine uses the verb *coagulare*, "coagulate."

7. Every teacher in the history of the church agrees. During the middle ages, for instance, the church developed the idea of "baptism of desire," which means that one can enjoy the benefits of baptism without baptism itself, if one desires baptism but is prevented from being baptized.

8. Irenaeus, *Against the Heresies* 1.8.1.

9. Christian teachers often compare and contrast Israel's rituals (like circumcision) with the Christian rite of baptism. According to Thomas Aquinas, circumcision removed a bit of skin, while baptism strips off the flesh that works immorality, impurity, idolatry, strife, anger, and envy. Circumcision was for Israel alone, while baptism is for all nations. Baptism is universal because it contains the "perfection of salvation," while circumcision signified the perfection that would come through the Jewish Messiah. Circumcision bestowed grace, but not as baptism

does. Circumcision foreshadowed a future passion. Baptism's superior power flows from Christ's finished passion (*Summa Theologiae* 3.70.1–4).

10. Jean Danielou, *The Bible and the Liturgy* (South Bend, IN: University of Notre Dame Press, 1956). Medieval scholastics are less poetic, but they discuss the "Sacraments of the Old Law" before examining the "Sacraments of the New Law." Protestants follow a similar method using the categories of old and new covenants.

11. Augustine, *Answer to Faustus* 19.16. See my "Conjugating the Rites: Old and New in Augustine's Theory of Signs," *Calvin Theological Journal* 34 (1999): 136–47.

12. Robert Kolb, *Making Disciples, Baptizing: God's Gift of New Life and Christian Witness* (St Louis: Concordia Seminary, 1997), 13. Luther notes that circumcision is sometimes called "covenant," and he concludes baptism can be described as "new covenant." Circumcision was a "sign or covenant (*signum seu pactum*) entrusted to Abraham" (quoted in Jonathan D. Trigg, *Baptism in the Theology of Martin Luther* [Leiden: Brill, 1994], 39).

13. Gregory of Nyssa, *On the Baptism of Christ*. Writing in *Against the Donatists* (5), fourth-century bishop Optatus says baptism cannot be repeated because God himself does the washing. Fifth-century bishop of Constantinople John Chrysostom says the whole Trinity acts in baptism (*Baptismal Homilies* 2.26). Many writers make the same point.

14. The technical term for this is *ex opera operato*, "by the work worked," though I am using the phrase in an unusual sense. Most Protestants reject the view that baptism is effective *ex opere operato*, insisting the baptized aren't automatically saved but must receive Jesus in faith. Historically, though, the phrase has other meanings. For Augustine, *ex opere operato* is an anti-Donatist motto: baptism's validity doesn't depend on the moral character of the minister who baptizes (*On Baptism, Against the Donatists*). Most Protestants agree with Augustine on that point. Most also affirm *ex opere operato* in other respects, too. Though Luther rejects the phrase, Trigg observes that he often writes as if baptism's effect is "automatic" (Trigg, *Baptism in the Theology of Martin Luther*, 77), and Reformed Protestants believe the rite of baptism automatically makes

us members of the "visible church." See my *Priesthood of the Plebs: A Theology of Baptism* (Eugene, OR: Wipf & Stock, 2003), 158–60.

15. *Institutes* 4.17.10.

16. Heinrich Bullinger makes the point strongly: "We openly profess that we have sacraments which are holy, and not profane; effectual, and not without force; garnished from above, not naked; and therefore they are full, not void or empty" (*Decades, Fifth Decade*, Sermon 8). According to Bullinger, God instituted the sacraments for the godly, and for the godly they are effective.

17. *Heidelberg Catechism*, Lord's Day 25, q. 66; *Westminster Confession of Faith* 27.1. The term is ancient. Ephrem the Syrian compares baptismal anointing and the Spirit to the seal of an official's signet ring (*Hymns* 7.6). Baptism is sometimes a seal, sometimes the means by which the Spirit seals our souls (2 Cor 1:22; Eph 1:13; 4:30). For the latter, see Cyril of Jerusalem, *Mystagogical Lectures* 16.24. See Jean Danielou, *The Bible and the Liturgy*, ch. 3.

18. Gregory Nazianzen wrote, "A sheep that is sealed is not easily snared, but that which is unmarked is an easy prey to thieves" (*Oration 40, on Baptism* 15).

19. Ambrose of Milan: "Slaves are marked with the sign of their master" (quoted in Danielou, *Bible and Liturgy*, 59).

20. The newly baptized, writes Gregory Nazianzen, is "like a young soldier who has just been given a place among the athletes, but has not yet proved his worth as a solider" (quoted in Danielou, *Bible and Liturgy*, 58).

21. Some churches administer baptism at Easter to coordinate the timing with the meaning of baptism. Easter baptism wasn't the norm prior to the fourth century, nor was it ever the norm everywhere. See Robin M. Jensen, *Baptismal Imagery in Early Christianity: Ritual, Visual, and Theological Dimensions* (Grand Rapids: Baker, 2012), 172–75. For general cautions about universalizing local liturgical custom, see Paul Bradshaw, *In Search for the Origins of Christian Worship: Sources and Methods for the Study of Early Liturgy* (Oxford: Oxford University Press, 2002).

22. Tertullian (*On Baptism* 2) urges us to respect "the antiquity of the waters," which are "the resting place of the Spirit of God, more pleasing to him

at that time than the other elements." He adds, "God's ordering of the world was in a sort of way carried out by regulative waters." See also *Teaching of Gregory*, 412.

23. Tertullian, *On Baptism* 3.

24. Tertullian, *On Baptism* 2.

25. Ambrose, *Sacraments* 3.3. So Tertullian (*On Baptism*, 1): "We, being little fishes, as Jesus Christ is our great Fish, begin our life in the water, and only while we abide in the water are we safe and sound." For the early Christians, the Greek word for fish, *ichthus*, was an acronym for *Iesous Christos, theou uios soter*, "Jesus Christ, Son of God, Savior." "Imitate the Fish" means "follow Jesus."

26. Masaru Emoto, *Secret Life of Water* (New York: ATRIA Books, 2011).

27. Tertullian, *On Baptism* 9.

28. Alick Bartholomew, *The Spiritual Life of Water* (Rochester, VT: Park Street Press, 2010), 24.

29. Narsai, *Homilies*, 370. For Theodore of Mopsuestia, sinners are hardened pots that need to be moistened with water in order to be reshaped (*Baptismal Homilies* 3.13).

30. Bartholomew, *Spiritual Life of Water*, 102–3.

31. Masaru Emoto, *The Hidden Messages of Water* (New York: ATRIA Books, 2005).

32. Solomon sponsors seafaring trading ventures, anticipating the new covenant (1 Kgs 9:26; 10:22). Jehoshaphat tries to imitate him but fails (1 Kgs 22:48).

33. Noah is the chief Old Testament exception.

34. Even today, the open ocean is untamed. See William Langewiesche, *The Outlaw Sea: A World of Freedom, Chaos, and Crime* (New York: North Point Press, 2004).

35. See Karl Wittfogel's controversial thesis about hydraulic societies in *Oriental Despotism: A Comparative Study of Total Power* (New Haven: Yale, 1957).

36. As Gregory of Nyssa put it, baptism binds together a world disrupted by sin, so that "the creation in the world and above the world, that once was at variance with itself, is knit together in friendship: and we men

are made to join in the angels' song, offering the worship of their praise to God" (*On the Baptism of Christ*).

37. Cyril, *Mystagogical Lectures* 1.9; see also *Odes of Solomon* 11.

38. The imagery comes from Melito of Sardis, Fragment B of *On Baptism*, who compares Jesus' baptism to the daily "bath" of the sun.

39. Tertullian, *On Baptism* 5.

40. "Baptismal regeneration" is the language of the universal church. See Cyril, *Mystagogical Lectures* 3.5; Ambrose, *Sacraments* 3.2–3; Theodore of Mopsuetsia, *Baptismal Homilies* 3.3; Augustine, *Enchiridion* 8.42. The font is a womb (Ephrem, *Hymn* 7.8; Narsai, *Homilies* 295; Theodore, *Baptismal Homilies* 3.9), which brings the baptized to a second birth (Novatian, *Trinity* 29.16). Zeno (*Invitations* 1, 3, 7) extends the metaphor to encourage the newborn to drink milk from their new mother. In early Christian art, the newly baptized were often depicted as naked children, newborn of the virgin mother church (Jensen, *Baptismal Imagery*, 56). Luther retains "regeneration" (Trigg, *Baptism in the Theology of Martin Luther*, 77), as does, more surprisingly, Calvin's mentor Martin Bucer (see Bucer's post-baptismal prayer in Hughes Oliphant Old, *The Shaping of the Reformed Baptismal Rite in the Sixteenth Century* [Grand Rapids: Eerdmans, 1992]). Both the Book of Common Prayer and the Catholic rite of baptism speak of baptismal "new birth."

41. Tertullian, *On Baptism* 8.

42. John Chrysostom sees the details as types of the gospel: "The ark is the church; Noe, Christ; the dove, the Holy Spirit; the olive branch, divine goodness. As in the midst of the sea, the ark protected those who were inside it, so the Church saves those who are spared. But the ark only protected, the Church does more. ... The Church takes in men without *logos* and does not merely protect them, she transforms them" (*Hom. Laz.* 6; quoted in Danielou, *Bible and the Liturgy*, 84).

43. Luther, *Small Catechism*.

44. The phrase comes from Chrysostom.

45. "Ark" occurs twenty-six times in the flood story, and twenty-six is the numerical value of YHWH. Yahweh is Noah's ark!

46. See Justin (*Dialogue with Trypho* 138.2): "wood, containing the mystery of the cross; even as Noah was saved by wood when he rode over the waters with his household."

47. Cyril of Jerusalem calls Jesus "the true Noe, the Author of the second birth" (*Mystagogical Lectures* 17.10).

48. According to Cyprian (*Epistle* 75), 1 Peter shows the "one Ark of Noah was a type of the one Church." Didymus the Blind (*On Baptism* 2) agreed the ark is "an image of the awe-inspiring church" (quoted in Danielou, *Bible and Liturgy*, 83).

49. The Bible sometimes depicts the sea as the abode of the dead (for example, Jonah 2:1–10).

50. Luther, quoted in *Make Disciples, Baptizing*, 86.

51. Kolb, *Make Disciples, Baptizing*, 70.

52. The Hebrew word for this offering, *ólah*, is from the verb *álah*, "go up." "Ascension offering" is a more accurate translation than "whole burnt offering." See L. Michael Morales, *Who Shall Ascend to the Mountain of the Lord? A Biblical Theology of the Book of Leviticus* (Downers Grove, IL: IVP, 2016), 135; James B. Jordan, *The Whole Burnt Sacrifice: Its Liturgy and Meaning* (Niceville, FL: Biblical Horizons, 1991).

53. There is a hint here of the liturgical sequence from baptism to Eucharist.

54. Justin, *Dialogue with Trypho* 138.2. Asterius draws the same comparison ("Sermon on Psalm 6," cited in Danielou, *Bible and Liturgy*, 80). Ancient baptisteries are often octagonal, to represent the eight-ness of baptism. See Jensen, *Baptismal Imagery*, 204–9; Garry Wills, *Font of Life: Ambrose, Augustine, and the Mystery of Baptism* (Oxford: Oxford University Press, 2012), 3–14.

55. Gregory of Nyssa (*On the Baptism of Christ*), Ambrose (*On the Sacraments* 1.10), and Tertullian (*On Baptism* 2) warn against despising the simplicity of baptism.

56. *Shepherd of Hermas* 11.1.

57. The pattern recurs at the end of Ruth, where David is the tenth after Judah (Ruth 4:18–22).

58. See N. T. Wright, *The Climax of the Covenant: Christ and the Law in Pauline Theology* (Minneapolis: Fortress Press, 1991), 21–23.

59. It is a long-standing opinion. Paul's warning to the Jews can be applied to a Christian "who has become a true Jew through faith in Christ and the circumcision given in baptism" (Origen, *Commentary on the Epistle to the Romans*, on 2:11). See Gregory Nazianzen, *Oration 40, on Baptism* 28. Calvin writes, "Just as circumcision, which was a kind of badge to the Jews, assuring them that they were adopted as the people and family of God, was their first entrance into the Church ... so now we are initiated by baptism, so as to be enrolled among his people, and at the same time swear unto his name" (*Institutes* 4.16.4). He cites Colossians 2:11–12 in support, arguing that "baptism is the same thing to Christians that circumcision formerly was to the Jews" (*Institutes* 4.16.11).

60. Asterius of Amasea says circumcision teaches Christians to "mark their children with the seal by Baptism in the circumcision of Christ" ("Homily on Psalm 6," quoted in Danielou, *Bible and Liturgy* [South Bend, IN: University of Notre Dame Press, 1956], 64–65). Augustine doesn't mention circumcision, but says that none, including infants and the aged, should be barred from baptism (*Enchiridion* 8.43). Calvin argues, "If the covenant remains firm and fixed, it is no less applicable to the children of Christians in the present day, than to the children of the Jews under the Old Testament. Now, if they are partakers of the thing signified, how can they be denied the sign? If they obtain the reality, how can they be refused the figure?" (*Institutes* 4.16.5).

    For recent discussions of the history of infant baptism, see Everett Ferguson, *Baptism in the Early Church: History, Theology, and Liturgy in the First Five Centuries* (Grand Rapids: Eerdmans, 2009), ch. 23; David F. Wright, *Infant Baptism in Historical Perspective* (Eugene, OR: Wipf & Stock, 2007). I'm convinced infant baptism was practiced in the apostolic age, though baptismal liturgies were designed for older candidates. See my "Infant Baptism in History: An Unfinished Tragicomedy," in *The Case for Covenantal Infant Baptism*, ed. Gregg Strawbridge (Phillipsburg, NJ: P&R Publishing, 2003), 246–62.

61. The early church was aware of its status as a "third race" alongside Jews, Greeks, and Romans. Mathetes's *Epistle to Diognetus* (1) contrasts Greeks and Jews to "this new group (*genos*) and their practices." Depending on the recension of his *Apology* (2), Aristides enumerates three or four

classes of men—Barbarians, Greeks, Jews, and Christians; or idolaters, Jews, and Christians. For discussion, see Judith Lieu, *Neither Jew nor Greek? Constructing Early Christianity* (London: Bloomsbury, 2015), 70–73.

62. N. T. Wright, *Colossians and Philemon* (Downers Grove, IL: InterVarsity Press, 2008), 109–11.

63. Following Mark 10:38–39, Tertullian calls Jesus' death a baptism in blood (*On Baptism* 6).

64. Church fathers compare the removal of the garment to the removal of Adam's animal skins (Gen 3:20). It's a return to the primal innocence of shameless nakedness. Some remind the baptized that Jesus was stripped naked on the cross (see Gregory of Nyssa, *On the Baptism of Christ*; Cyril, *Mystagogical Lectures* 2.2).

65. Tertullian, *On Baptism* 9; Cyril of Jerusalem, *Mystagogical Lectures* 1.2–3.

66. See Peter Sabo, "Drawing Out Moses: Water as a Personal Motif of the Biblical Character," in *Thinking of Water in the Early Second Temple Period*, ed. Ehud Ben Zvi and Christoph Levin (Berlin: Walter de Gruyter, 2014), 410–36.

67. The Hebrew word for Noah's "ark" is *tevah*, and the only use outside the flood story is with reference to the basket in which Moses floats down the Nile (Exod 2:2–3). Moses lives in the twenty-sixth generation of humanity, and twenty-six is the numerical value of YHWH, the name of Israel's God. See note 45.

68. Sabo notes that "Moses" is active, not passive; it means "he draws out," not "he is drawn out" ("Drawing Out Moses," 416). "Moses" more looks forward to the exodus than backward to his birth.

69. Gregory of Nyssa sees Moses' rescue from the Nile as a baptism (*On the Baptism of Christ*), albeit without taking note of Moses' age.

70. The Hebrew *chasaq* is typically translated as "harden," but "strengthen" is the usual meaning. Yahweh doesn't force Pharaoh to be resistant; Yahweh strengthens and uplifts Pharaoh's heart so that he thinks he's invulnerable. See David Fohrman, *The Exodus You Almost Passed Over* (New York: Aleph Beta Press, 2016).

71. Tertullian, *On Baptism* 9. Some contrast unchosen natural birth to the willed second birth of baptism. Baptism is a passage from necessity to choice. See Justin, *First Apology* 61; Theodotus, *Excepta* 78.

72. Cyril of Jerusalem, *Catechetical Lectures* 19.3; the church father Origen agrees, *Homilies on Exodus* 5.5.

73. Basil, *On the Holy Spirit* 14.

74. See H. A. Kelly, *The Devil at Baptism: Ritual, Theology, and Drama* (Eugene, OR: Wipf & Stock, 2004). See Cyril of Jerusalem, *Mystagogical Lectures* 1.6–7; John Chrysostom, *Baptismal Homilies* 2.23; Cyprian, *Epistle* 68. For Theodore of Mopsuestia, the devil's angels are heretics who trouble the faithful (*Baptismal Homilies* 2.8). Exorcism is part of Western initiation during the Middle Ages (Hugh, *On the Sacraments*, 298; see the thirteenth-century *Metz Pontifical*, excerpted in Peter Cramer, "Baptismal Practice in Germany," in *Medieval Religion in Practice*, ed. Miri Rubin [Princeton: Princeton University Press, 2009], 7–8). Exorcisms and renunciations remain in modern baptismal liturgies.

75. Quoted in Danielou, *Bible and Liturgy*, 94.

76. Alexander Schmemann, *Of Water and the Spirit* (Crestwood, NY: St. Vladimir's Seminary Press, 1997), 29–30.

77. Early Christian writer Theodotus emphasizes that Jesus is "troubled" after baptism (*Excerpta* 85).

78. Ephrem sees the incident at Marah as a type of baptism (*Hymn for Epiphany* 4), and Tertullian sees the tree as a type of the life-giving cross (*On Baptism* 9).

79. The Spirit is present in the form of a cloud. Origen says that Paul's typological reading of the exodus is simply a restatement of Jesus' words: "Unless a man is born again of water and the Spirit, he cannot enter the kingdom of heaven" (Origen, *Homilies on Exodus* 5.1). Ambrose elaborated the cloud-Spirit connection: "The people were in the sea and the column of light went ahead, then the column of a cloud followed like the shadow of the Holy Spirit. You see that by the Holy Spirit and by the water He displayed a figure of baptism" (*On the Sacraments* 1.22). As light, the cloud points to the illuminating power of baptism: "What is a column of light but the Lord Christ, who has dispelled the shadows of infidelity, has infused the light of truth and grace into human inclinations" (*On the Sacraments* 1.22).

80. See Wright, "New Exodus, New Inheritance: The Narrative Substructure of Romans 3–8," in *Romans and the People of God: Essays in Honor of Gordon D. Fee on the Occasion of His 65th Birthday*, eds. S. Soderlund and N. T. Wright (Grand Rapids: Eerdmans, 1999), 26–35.

81. All major English translations render *typoi* here as "examples."

82. Robert Kolb, *Make Disciples, Baptizing*, 57. Kolb is exegeting Peter's exhortation in Acts 2.

83. Luther, Sermon on May 29, 1528, WA 30,1:22.1. See *Disputation on the Power and Efficacy of Indulgences* (1517), LW 31:25.

84. See Matthew W. Bates, *Salvation by Allegiance Alone: Rethinking Faith, Works, and the Gospel of Jesus the King* (Grand Rapids: Baker, 2017). *Sacramentum* originally meant "pledge of loyalty" or "oath of allegiance." See Jensen, *Baptismal Imagery*, 66.

85. Augustine cites the unjust steward to explain what happens to merciless Christians (*On Baptism* 12.19).

86. Cyril of Jerusalem, *Mystagogical Lectures* 1.8. Origen warns that some revert from baptism (*Homilies on Joshua* 4.2).

87. Theodore says the candidate pledges to "stand form and unshakable at God's side" and "never on any account abandon him" (*Baptismal Homilies* 2.13). See Chrysostom on the baptismal "contract" (*Baptismal Homilies* 2.17).

88. For a more developed discussion of this point, see my *Delivered from the Elements of the World: Atonement, Justification, Mission* (Downers Grove: IVP Academic, 2016), 94–97.

89. The most systematic defense of infant communion is Tim Gallant, *Feed My Lambs: Why the Lord's Table Should Be Restored to Covenant Children* (Grande Prairie, Alberta: Pactum Reformanda, 2002). In the Orthodox churches, infants receive a taste of communion immediately after baptism. Infant or young child communion is practiced in some Anglican and Presbyterian churches.

90. See Richard Beck, *Unclean: Meditations on Purity, Hospitality, and Morality* (Cambridge, UK: Lutterworth Press, 2012).

91. John Paul II, *Man and Woman He Created Them: A Theology of the Body* (Boston: Pauline Books, 2006), 12.2.

92. Cyril of Jerusalem, *Mystagogical Lectures* 2.2.

93. Ephrem, *Hymn* 7.5–6. See also Tertullian, *On Baptism* 7; Cyril of Jerusalem, *Mystagogical Lectures* 3.6; Ambrose, *On the Sacraments* 1.2. See my *Priesthood of the Plebs: A Theology of Baptism* (Eugene, OR: Wipf & Stock, 2003), and the eccentric but intriguing discussion of the "covenant with Levi" in Douglas van Dorn, *Waters of Creation* (Eerie, CO: Waters of Creation Publishing, 2009).

94. For the church fathers, baptismal anointing makes one a partaker of Jesus Christ the olive tree (Cyril of Jerusalem, *Catechetical Lectures* 20.3), heals (*Euchology* of Serapion, quoted in Danielou, *Bible and Liturgy*, 39), and prepares us for athletic combat (Pseudo-Dionysius, *Ecclesiastical Hierarchy* 3.6).

95. The Shepherd of Hermas imagines each living stone rising to its place on a baptismal wave (*Shepherd of Hermas* 2.5.1).

96. Nahum Sarna, *Exploring Exodus: The Origins of Biblical Israel* (New York: Schocken, 2006), 203–4; L. Michael Morales, *The Tabernacle Pre-Figured: Cosmic Mountain Ideology in Genesis and Exodus* (Leuven: Peeters, 2012); Morales, *Who Shall Ascend*, 94–100.

97. See especially Morales, *Tabernacle Pre-Figured*, 1–50.

98. Trigg, *Baptism in the Theology of Martin Luther*, 30–37, 177. For Chrysostom, baptismal exorcisms are spiritual housecleaning, purging the soul for the arrival of the King (*Baptismal Homilies* 2.12).

99. Deuteronomy 12 teaches that Yahweh required Israel to seek him at a single sanctuary. Luther applies this text to baptism, one of the places God may be found (Trigg, *Baptism in the Theology of Martin Luther*, 25). For Luther, God is always found where promises to be found: in his word, in baptism, in Communion, and in absolution.

100. This is one of Luther's earliest Reformation battle cries. See *The Babylonian Captivity of the Church*, LW 36:11–126.

101. See Dale Allison, *The New Moses: A Matthean Typology* (Eugene, OR: Wipf & Stock, 2013), 23–28.

102. Ephrem speaks of the "womb" of the Jordan (*On Christ as Light* 3). According to Origen, the Red Sea crossing was a baptism of "law," but the passage through the Jordan is a baptism of gospel (*Homilies on Joshua* 5–6).

103. Water seems weak, but it is not. As the *Tao Te Ching* (78) puts it,

> Under heaven nothing is more soft and yielding than water.
> Yet for attacking the solid and strong, nothing is better;
> It has no equal.
> The weak can overcome the strong;
> The supple can overcome the stiff.
> Under heaven everyone knows this,
> Yet no one puts it into practice.

(Translation by Gia-Fu Fent and Jane English. London: Wildwood House, 1991.

104. N. T. Wright, *Jesus and the Victory of God,* The New Testament and the Question of God 2 (Minneapolis: Fortress, 1996).

105. Whatever his connection with the Essenes, John echoes their theology. Believing Israel had become corrupt and that the priesthood was illegitimate, they left the land for Qumran, reenacting the story of Joshua in reverse. But they expected eventually to pass triumphantly through the Jordan back into the land.

106. Cyril of Jerusalem, *Catechetical Lectures* 10.11; Aphrahat, *Demonstrations* 11.12. "Do you wish to learn again which battles, which wars, await us after baptism?" Origen asks, and answers by citing Paul's list of spiritual armor and giving a pep talk: "Why delay? Let us go forth to the war, so that we may subdue the chief city of this world, malice, and destroy the proud walls of sin. You look around, by chance, for the road you must take, which field of battle to seek after. ... You require nothing from without, beyond your own self; within you is the battle" (*Homilies on Joshua* 5).

107. Origen pushes the connection to the point that he identifies the river with the Word: "We must ... understand by the Jordan the Word of God made flesh Who dwelt among us, and by Jesus (Joshua) who distributed the shares, the humanity that He assumed" (quoted in Danielou, *Bible and Liturgy,* 103). Novatian, *Trinity* 29.16, stresses the Spirit as the pledge of the inheritance of the baptized.

108. To symbolize that we already enjoy the heavenly Canaan, the newly baptized sometimes eat milk and honey. Jensen, *Baptismal Imagery,* 122–27; Ferguson, *Baptism in the Early Church,* 213, 315–16, 333. See *Odes of Solomon* 19. Gregory of Nyssa mentions milk and honey while drawing

out the parallels between entry into the land and reentry to Paradise: "You have been for a long time wallowing in the mud: hasten to the Jordan, not at the call of John, but at the voice of Christ. In fact the river of grace runs everywhere. It does not rise in Palestine to disappear in the neighboring sea; but it envelops the entire world and plunges itself into Paradise, flowing against the course of the four rivers which come down from thence, and carrying back into Paradise things far more precious than those which came out. For those rivers brought sweet perfumes, and the cultivation and semination of the earth: but this river brings back men, born of the Holy Spirit. Imitate Jesus, the son of Nave. Carry the Gospel as he carried the Ark. Leave the desert, that is to say, sin. Cross the Jordan. Hasten toward Life according to Christ, toward the earth which bears the fruits of joy, where run, according to the promise, streams of milk and honey" (quoted in Danielou, *Bible and Liturgy*, 101–2).

109. In many hymns, "crossing Jordan" refers to death's passage into heaven. For instance: "When I tread the verge of Jordan, / Bid my anxious fears subside. / Death of death, / and hell's Destruction, / Land me safe on Canaan's side" (William Williams, "Guide Me, O Thou Great Jehovah," 1745).

110. See John Chrysostom, *Baptismal Homilies* 2.1, 22. In some liturgies, baptism was followed by an enrollment ceremony with military overtones (Jensen, *Baptismal Imagery*, 83–84). See Basil, *Exhortation* 7.

111. Gregory of Nyssa spiritualizes the conquest of Jericho: the old city that must be conquered is the flesh (*On the Baptism of Christ*). Gregory is right, but our flesh isn't the only field of battle.

112. See *The Freedom of a Christian*, LW 31:333–77.

113. *The Freedom of a Christian*, LW 31:344. Our lordship isn't domination but love. "When you love men," Thomas Traherne says, "the world quickly becometh yours." Those you love are "your treasures, and all things in Heaven and Earth that serve them, are yours" (*Centuries of Meditations*, ed. Bertram Dobell [New York: Cosimo Classics, 2007], 2.64).

114. Theodore of Mopsuestia takes John 3:5 as a baptismal text. Jesus "mentioned water because it is in water that the work is accomplished" and "he mentioned Spirit because the Spirit exercises its power through

the water." Water is the "womb," while the Spirit is "the real agent" of the "regeneration" that occurs in baptism. Anyone who passes through baptismal death and resurrection "is said to be born again" (*Commentary on the Gospel of John*, at 3:5). Some baptismal liturgies include an epiclesis, an invocation calling on the Spirit to "impregnate" the womb of the waters. See Danielou, *Bible and Liturgy* (South Bend, IN: Notre Dame University Press, 1956), 48.

115. According to the church doctor Jerome, "The Spirit of God above moved, as a charioteer, over the face of the waters ... and produced from them the infant world, a type of the Christian child that is drawn from the laver of baptism" (*Letters* 69.6).

116. Many writers link baptismal anointing with illumination. See Dionysus, *Ecclesiastical Hierarchy* 3; *Odes of Solomon* 11. Ambrose links initiation to Jesus' "anointing" the eyes of the man born blind (John 9:11), which gives him sight (*On the Sacraments* 3.13).

117. For summaries, see Jensen, *Baptismal Imagery*, 40–42, 106–10; Ferguson, *Baptism in the Early Church*, 353–54, 426–27. See *Gelasian Sacramentary* 1.40; Hugh, *On the Sacraments*, 299. Jensen shows that early baptisms included no anointings (*Baptismal Imagery*, 96–97). I share the Reformers' objections to extraneous rites. The biblical rite is a bath or shower in water, and introducing other rites introduces confusion. This is no theoretical concern. Confirmation is one example. It developed as a separate rite when anointing was detached from initiation. For all its possible benefits, confirmation often raises doubts about the efficacy of baptism. See J. D. C. Fisher, *Christian Initiation: Confirmation Then and Now* (Mundelein, IL: Hillenbrand Books, [1978] 2007).

118. Ephrem (*Hymns* 7.13) and Cyril (*Mystagogical Lectures* 2.3, 3.1) say that anointing links us to Christ the olive tree, so that we become "christs." Anointing with oil is connected, in diverse ways, with the anointing of the Spirit (Cyril, *Mystagogical Lectures* 3.1–2). Candidates are oiled up, like athletes ready for the arena (Ambrose, *On Sacraments* 1.4). It is the oil of gladness (Cyril, *Mystagogical Lectures* 3.2) and a perfume that makes us aromatic with the fragrance of Christ.

119. Note the parallels with the Spirit-filled servant of Isaiah 11, who brings justice, rescues the oppressed, liberates prisoners, reconciles wild and tame, and makes the land spring up with righteousness and peace.

120. Justin emphasizes that the rich and poor both receive the blessing of baptism (*First Apology* 6–7).

121. See the hymn of Prudentius in Jensen, *Baptismal Imagery*, 68–69.

122. Cyprian emphasizes that the Spirit falls on both men and women (*Epistle* 69.14).

123. Leo, *Epistle* 16.

124. Abraham Heschel, *The Prophets* (Peabody, MA: Hendrickson, 2007).

125. Quoted in Danielou, *Bible and Liturgy* (South Bend, IN: Notre Dame University Press, 1956), 106.

126. Gregory of Nyssa, *On the Baptism of Christ*. See Ambrose, *On the Sacraments* 2.11.

127. Origen, *Commentary on the Gospel According to John* 6.238. Cyril of Jerusalem makes the same connection, but he sets it in a broader context. "Where a covenant is made with any, there is water also. After the flood, a covenant was made with Noah: a covenant from Mount Sinai, but *with water, and scarlet wool, and hyssop*. ... Elias is taken up, but not apart from water: for first he crosses the Jordan, then in a chariot mounts the heaven" (*Catechectical Lectures* 3.5).

128. Justin the Martyr says, "Christ, by being crucified on the tree, and by purifying [us] with water, has redeemed us" (Justin, *Dialogue with Trypho*, 86). Didymus the Blind agrees: "By the wood taken and thrown into the place where lay the object of the search is symbolized the glorious Cross. The Jordan is immortal Baptism. ... The iron which floated on the waters and came back to him who had lost it, signifies that we mount by Baptism to a heavenly height and find again the grace of our old and true home country" (quoted in Danielou, *Bible and Liturgy*, 108).

129. Raymond B. Dillard, *Faith in the Face of Apostasy: The Gospel According to Elijah and Elisha* (Phillipsburg, NJ: P&R, 1999), 121–26.

130. Origen, *Commentary on the Gospel of John* 6.244. See Ambrose: "In my opinion his leprosy of soul was purified just as much as his leprosy of body; because immediately after his plunge into the water, on seeing himself utterly free of the marks of his disease, he exclaimed that he

would no longer pour out libations to foreign gods, but would offer sacrifice to none but the Lord" (*Commentary on the Gospel of Luke* 4.51). See also Ephrem, *Hymns for Epiphany* 1.3.

131. In the early church, candidates were often stripped and baptized naked. After being washed and anointed, they received a prophetic robe of dazzling white and became the marvel of angels. See Ambrose, *On the Sacraments* 4.5.

TRANSLATIONS USED

Ambrose. *Commentary of Saint Ambrose on the Gospel according to Saint Luke*. Translated by Ide M. Ni Riain. Dublin: Halcyon Press, 2001.

———. *The Mysteries*. In Ambrose, *Theological and Dogmatic Works*. Fathers of the Church 44. Translated by Roy J. Deferrari. Washington, DC: Catholic University of America Press, 1963.

———. *On the Sacraments*. In Ambrose, *Theological and Dogmatic Works*. Fathers of the Church 44. Translated by Roy J. Deferrari. Washington, DC: Catholic University of America Press, 1963.

Aphrahat. *Demonstrations*. In Philip Schaff and Henry Wace, eds., Nicene and Post-Nicene Fathers, 2nd ser., vol. 13. Translated by John Gwynn. Buffalo, NY: Christian Literature Publishing, 1980.

Aquinas, Thomas. *Summa Theologiae: A Concise Translation*. 5 vols. Translated by Fathers of English Dominican Province. Allen, TX: Christian Classics, [1948] 1981.

Aristides. *Apology*. In Allan Menzies, ed., Ante-Nicene Fathers 9. Translated by D. M. Kay. Buffalo, NY: Christian Literature Publishing, 1896.

Augustine. *Answer to Faustus, A Manichean*. In *Works of St. Augustine: A Translation for the 21st Century*. Translated by Elizabeth Ruth Obbard. Hyde Park, NY: New City Press, 2007.

BAPTISM

———. *On Baptism, against the Donatists*. In Philip Schaff, ed., Nicene and Post-Nicene Fathers, 1st ser., vol. 4. Translated by J. R. King. Buffalo, NY: Christian Literature Publishing, 1887.

———. *Enchiridion*. In Augustine, *Confessions and Enchiridion*. Library of Christian Classics 7. Translated by Albert C. Outler. Louisville: Westminster Press, 1955.

Basil the Great. *Exhortation to Baptism*. In Basil, *A Treatise on Baptism; With an Exhortation to Receive It*. Translated by Francis Patrick Kenrick. Philadelphia: M. Fithian, 1843.

———. *On the Holy Spirit*. In Basil, *The Treatise of St. Basil the Great*. Christian Classics Series 4. Translated by George Lewis. London: Religious Tract Society, 1888.

Bullinger, Henry. *The Decades of Henry Bullinger*. 4 vols. Translated by H. I. Cambridge: Cambridge University Press, 1849–1852.

Calvin, John. *Institutes of the Christian Religion*. 2 vols. Library of Christian Classics. Translated by Ford Lewis Battles. Louisville, KY: Westminster John Knox Press, 1960.

Cyprian. *Epistle 69*. In Cyprian, *Letters (1–81)*. Fathers of the Church 51. Translated by Rose Bernard Donna. Washington, DC: Catholic University of American Press, 1964.

Cyril of Jerusalem. *Catechetical Lectures*. Philip Schaff and Henry Wace, eds., Nicene and Post-Nicene Fathers, 2nd ser., vol. 7. Translated by Edwin Hamilton Gifford. Buffalo, NY: Christian Literature Publishing, 1894.

———. *Mystagogical Lectures*. In Cyril, *Works, vol. 2*. Fathers of the Church 64. Translated by Leo P. McCauley and Anthony A. Stephenson. Washington, DC: Catholic University of America Press, 1970.

Dionysius. *Ecclesiastical Hierarchy*. In Dionysius, *The Ecclesiastical Hierarchy*. Studies in Sacred Theology, 2nd ser., vol. 83. Translated by Thomas L. Campbell. Washington: Catholic University of America Press, 1955.

Ephrem. *On Christ as Light in Mary and Jordan*. Sebastian Brock, trans., "St. Ephrem on Christ as Light in Mary and in the Jordan: Hymni de Ecclesia 36." *Eastern Churches Review* 7 (1975): 137–44.

———. *Hymns*. In Sebastian Brock, trans., *The Harp of the Spirit: Poems of Saint Ephrem the Syrian*. Cambridge, UK: Institute for Orthodox Christian Studies, 2013.

———. *Hymns for Epiphany*. In Thomas M. Finn, *Early Christian Baptism and the Catechumenate: West and East Syria*. Message of the Fathers of the Church 5. Translated by Sebastian Brock. Collegeville, MN: Liturgical Press, 1992.

Gelasian Sacramentary. In Thomas Finn, *Early Christian Baptism and the Catechumenate: Italy, North Africa, and Egypt*. Message of the Fathers of the Church 6. Collegeville, MN: Liturgical Press, 1992.

Gregory Nazianzen. *Oration 40, On Baptism*. Philip Schaff and Henry Wace, eds., Nicene and Post-Nicene Fathers, 2nd ser., vol. 7. Translated by Charles Gordon Browne and James Edward Swallow. Buffalo, NY: Christian Literature Publishing, 1894.

Gregory of Nyssa. *On the Baptism of Christ*. Philip Schaff and Henry Wace, eds., Nicene and Post-Nicene Fathers, 2nd ser., vol. 5. Translated by H. A. Wilson. Buffalo, NY: Christian Literature Publishing, 1893.

Hugh of Saint Victor. *On the Sacraments*. Translated by Roy Deferrari. Cambridge, MA: Mediaeval Academy of America, 1951.

Irenaeus. *Against the Heresies*. Translated by Dominic J. Unger. New York: Newman Press, 1992.

Jerome. *Letters*. Philip Schaff and Henry Wace, eds., Nicene and Post-Nicene Fathers, 2nd ser., vol. 6. Translated by W. H. Fremantle, G. Lewis and W. G. Martley. Buffalo: Christian Literature Publishing, 1893.

John Chrysostom. *Baptismal Homilies*. In Edward Yarnold, trans., *The Awe-Inspiring Rites of Initiation: Baptismal Homilies of the Fourth Century*. Middlegreen, Slough: St. Paul Publications, 1972.

Justin. *Dialogue with Trypho the Jew*. Alexander Roberts, et al., eds., Ante-Nicene Fathers 1. Translated by Marcus Dods and George Reith. Buffalo, NY: Christian Literature Publishing Co., 1885.

———. *First Apology*. In Justin, *Justin Martyr*. Fathers of the Church 6. Translated by Thomas B. Falls. Washington, DC: Catholic University of America Press, 1948.

Leo the Great. *Epistle 16 to Sicilian*. In Leo, *Letters*. Fathers of the Church 34. Translated by Edmund Hunt. Washington, DC: Catholic University of American Press, 1957.

Luther, Martin. *The Babylonian Captivity of the Church*. In Luther, *Three Treatises*. Translated by A. T. W. Steinhauser. Philadelphia: Fortress Press, 1970.

———. *The Freedom of a Christian*. In Luther, *Three Treatises*. Translated by W. A. Lambert. Philadelphia: Fortress Press, 1970.

———. *Lectures on Genesis, Chapters 15–20*. Jaroslav Pelikan, ed., *Luther's Works*, vol. 3. Translated by George V. Schick. St. Louis: Concordia, 1986.

———. *Small Catechism*. St. Louis, MO: Concordia Publishing House, 1986.

Mathetes. *Epistle to Diognetus*. Alexander Roberts, et al., eds., Ante-Nicene Fathers 1. Translated by Alexander Roberts and James Donaldson. Buffalo, NY: Christian Literature Publishing, 1885.

Melito of Sardis. *On Baptism*. In Melito of Sardis, *On Pascha and Fragments*. Oxford Early Christian Texts. Translated by Stuart G. Hall. Oxford: Clarendon, 1979.

Narsai. *Metrical Homilies on the Nativity, Epiphany, Passion, Resurrection, and Ascension*. Patrologia Orientalis 182. Translated by Frederick G. McLeod. Turnhout, Belgium: Brepols, 1979.

Novatian. *The Trinity*. In Novatian, *The Trinity; The Spectacles: Jewish Foods; In Praise of Purity; Letters*. Fathers of the Church 67. Translated by Russell J. DeSimone. Washington, DC: Catholic University of America Press, 1972.

Odes of Solomon. In James H. Charlesworth, ed., *The Old Testament Pseudepigrapha*, vol. 2. Garden City: Doubleday, 1985.

Optatus. *Against Donatists*. In Optatus, *The Work of Saint Optatus Against the Donatists*. Translated by O. R. Vassall-Phillips. London: Longmans, Green, 1917.

Origen. *Commentary on the Epistle to the Romans, Books 1–5*. Fathers of the Church 103. Translated by Thomas P. Sheck. Washington, DC: Catholic University of America Press, 2009.

——. *Commentary on the Gospel of John, Books 1–10.* Fathers of the Church 80. Translated by Ronald E. Heine. Washington, DC: Catholic University of America Press, 1989.

——. *Homilies on Exodus.* In Origin, *Homilies on Genesis and Exodus.* Fathers of the Church 71. Translated by Ronald E. Heine. Washington, DC: Catholic University of America Press, 1982.

——. *Homilies on Joshua.* Fathers of the Church 105. Translated Barbara J. Bruce. Washington, DC: Catholic University of America Press, 2002.

Shepherd of Hermas. In *The Apostolic Fathers.* Fathers of the Church 1. Translated by Joseph M.-F. Marique. Washington, DC: Catholic University of America Press, 1947.

Tao Te Ching. Translated by Gia-Fu Fent and Jane English. London: Wildwood House, 1991.

Teaching of Gregory. In *The Teaching of Saint Gregory: An Early Armenian Catechism.* Harvard Armenian Texts and Studies 3. Translated by R. W. Thomson. Cambridge, MA: Harvard University Press, 1970.

Tertullian. *Homily on Baptism.* Translated by Ernest Evans. London: SPCK, 1964.

Theodore of Mopsuestia. *Baptismal Homilies.* In Edward Yarnold, trans., *The Awe-Inspiring Rites of Initiation: Baptismal Homilies of the Fourth Century.* Middlegreen, Slough: St. Paul Publications, 1972.

——. *Commentary on the Gospel of John.* Ancient Christian Texts. Edited by Joel C. Elowsky. Translated by Marco Conti. Downers Grove, IL: InterVarsity Press, 2010.

Theodotus. *Excerpta.* In Robert P. Casey, ed., *The Excerpta ex Theodoto of Clement of Alexandria.* London: Christophers, 1934.

Zeno of Verona. *Invitations to the Baptismal Font.* In A.-G. Hamann, ed., *Baptism: Ancient Liturgies and Patristic Texts.* Translated by Thomas Halton. Staten Island: Alba House, 1967.

WORKS CITED

Allison, Dale. *The New Moses: A Matthean Typology*. Eugene, OR: Wipf & Stock, 2013.

Bartholomew, Alick. *The Spiritual Life of Water: Its Power and Purpose*. Rochester, VT: Park Street Press, 2010.

Bates, Matthew W. *Salvation by Allegiance Alone: Rethinking Faith, Works, and the Gospel of Jesus the King*. Grand Rapids: Baker, 2017.

Beck, Richard. *Unclean: Meditations on Purity, Hospitality, and Morality*. Cambridge: Lutterworth Press, 2012.

Bradshaw, Paul. *In Search for the Origins of Christian Worship: Sources and Methods for the Study of Early Liturgy*. Oxford: Oxford University Press, 2002.

Cramer, Peter. "Baptismal Practice in Germany." In Miri Rubin, ed., *Medieval Religion in Practice*. Princeton Readings in Religion. Princeton: Princeton University Press, 2009.

Danielou, Jean. *The Bible and the Liturgy*. South Bend, IN: University of Notre Dame Press, 1956.

Dillard, Raymond B. *Faith in the Face of Apostasy: The Gospel According to Elijah & Elisha*. Phillipsburg, NJ: P&R, 1999.

Emoto, Masaru. *The Hidden Messages of Water*. New York: ATRIA Books, 2005.

———. *Secret Life of Water*. New York: ATRIA Books, 2011.

BAPTISM

Ferguson, Everett. *Baptism in the Early Church: History, Theology, and Liturgy in the First Five Centuries*. Grand Rapids: Eerdmans, 2009.

Finn, Thomas M. *Early Christian Baptism and the Catechumenate: West and East Syria*. Message of the Fathers of the Church 5. Collegeville, MN: Liturgical Press, 1992.

———. *Early Christian Baptism and the Catechumenate: Italy, North Africa, and Egypt*. Message of the Fathers of the Church 6. Collegeville, MN: Liturgical Press, 1992.

Fisher, J. D. C. *Christian Initiation: Confirmation Then and Now*. Chicago: Hillenbrand Books, [1978] 2005.

———. *Christian Initiation: The Reformation Period*. London: SPCK, 1970.

Fohrman, David. *The Exodus You Almost Passed Over*. New York: Alpha Beta Press, 2016.

Gallant, Tim. *Feed My Lambs: Why the Lord's Table Should Be Restored to Covenant Children*. Grande Prairie, Albert: Pactum Reformanda, 2002.

Heschel, Abraham. *The Prophets*. Peabody, MA: Hendrickson, 2007.

Jensen, Robin M. *Baptismal Imagery in Early Christianity*. Grand Rapids: Baker, 2012.

John Paul II. *Man and Woman He Created Them: A Theology of the Body*. Boston: Pauline Books, 2006.

———. *The Whole-Burnt Sacrifice: Its Liturgy and Meaning*. Biblical Horizons Occasional Paper 11. Niceville, FL: Biblical Horizons, 1991.

Kelly, H. A. *The Devil at Baptism: Ritual, Theology, and Drama*. Eugene, OR: Wipf & Stock, 2004.

Kolb, Robert. *Making Disciples, Baptizing: God's Gift of New Life and Christian Witness*. St. Louis, MO: Concordia Seminary, 1997.

Langewiesche, William. *The Outlaw Sea: A World of Freedom, Chaos, and Crime*. New York: North Point Press, 2004.

Leithart, Peter J. *The Baptized Body*. Moscow, Idaho: Canon Press, 2007.

———. "Conjugating the Rites: Old and New in Augustine's Theory of Signs." *Calvin Theological Journal* 34 (1999): 136–47.

———. *Delivered from the Elements of the World: Atonement, Justification, Mission*. Downers Grove, IL: InterVarsity Press, 2016.

———. "Infant Baptism in History: An Unfinished Tragicomedy." In Gregg Strawbridge, ed., *The Case for Covenantal Infant Baptism.* Phillipsburg, NJ: P&R Publishing, 2003.

———. *Priesthood of the Plebs: A Theology of Baptism.* Eugene, OR: Wipf & Stock, 2003.

Lieu, Judith. *Neither Jew nor Greek? Constructing Early Christianity.* London: Bloomsbury, 2015.

Morales, L. Michael. *The Tabernacle Pre-Figured: Cosmic Mountain Ideology in Genesis and Exodus.* Leuven: Peeters, 2012.

———. *Who Shall Ascend to the Mountain of the Lord? A Biblical Theology of the Book of Leviticus.* New Studies in Biblical Theology 37. Downers Grove, IL: InterVarsity Press, 2015.

Old, Hughes Oliphant. *The Shaping of the Reformed Baptismal Rite in the Sixteenth Century.* Grand Rapids: Eerdmans, 1992.

Sabo, Peter. "Drawing Out Moses: Water as a Personal Motif of the Biblical Character." In *Thinking of Water in the Early Second Temple Period,* edited by Ehud Ben Zvi and Christoph Levin, 409–36. Beihefte zur Zeitschrift fur die alttestamentliche Wissenschaft, Band 461. Berlin: Walter de Gruyter, 2014.

Sarna, Nahum. *Exploring Exodus: The Origins of Biblical Israel.* New York: Schocken, 2006.

Schmemann, Alexander. *Of Water and the Spirit: A Liturgical Study of Baptism.* Crestwood, NY: St. Vladimir's Seminary Press, 2001.

Traherne, Thomas. *Centuries of Meditation.* Bertram Dobell, ed. New York: Cosimo Classics, 2007.

Trigg, Jonathan D. *Baptism in the Theology of Martin Luther.* Studies in the History of Christian Thought 56. Leiden: Brill, 1994.

Van Dorn, Douglas. *Waters of Creation: A Biblical-Theological Study of Baptism.* Eerie, CO: Waters of Creation Publishing, 2009.

Wills, Garry. *Font of Life: Ambrose, Augustine, and the Mystery of Baptism.* Oxford: Oxford University Press, 2012.

Wittfogel, Karl. *Oriental Despotism: A Comparative Study of Total Power.* New Haven, CT: Yale University Press, 1957.

World Council of Churches. *Baptism, Eucharist, and Ministry*. Faith and Order Paper 111. Geneva: World Council of Churches, 1982.

Wright, David F. *Infant Baptism in Historical Perspective*. Eugene, OR: Wipf & Stock, 2007.

Wright, N. T. *The Climax of the Covenant*. Minneapolis: Fortress, 1993.

———. *Colossians and Philemon: An Introduction and Commentary*. Tyndale New Testament Commentaries 12. Downers Grove, IL: InterVarsity Academic, 2008.

———. *Jesus and the Victory of God*. The New Testament and the Question of God 2. Minneapolis: Fortress, 1996.

———. "New Exodus, New Inheritance: The Narrative Substructure of Romans 3–8." In S. Soderlund and N. T. Wright, eds., *Romans and the People of God: Essays in Honor of Gordon D. Fee on the Occasion of His 65th Birthday*. Grand Rapids: Eerdmans, 1999.

Yarnold, Edward. *The Awe-Inspiring Rites of Initiation: Baptismal Homilies of the Fourth Century*. Middlegreen, Slough: St. Paul Publications, 1972.

AUTHOR INDEX

SCRIPTURE INDEX

The Christian Essentials series is set in TEN OLDSTYLE, designed by Robert Slimbach in 2017. This typeface is inspired by Italian humanist and Japanese calligraphy, blending energetic formality with fanciful elegance.

CHRISTIAN ESSENTIALS

*The Christian Essentials series passes
down tradition that matters. The ancient
church was founded on basic biblical
teachings and practices like the Ten
Commandments, baptism, the Apostles'
Creed, the Lord's Supper, the Lord's Prayer,
and corporate worship. These basics of the
Christian life have sustained and nurtured
every generation of the faithful—from
the apostles to today. The books in the
Christian Essentials series open up the
meaning of the foundations of our faith.*